FLORIDA
LITERATURE
A Case Study

FLORIDA LITERATURE

A Case Study

With an Introduction by Carolina Hospital

BEDFORD/ST. MARTIN'S   Boston ◆ New York

For Bedford/St. Martin's

Executive Editor: Ellen Thibault
Developmental Editor: Christina Gerogiannis
Assistant Production Manager: Joe Ford
Marketing Manager: Stacey Propps
Executive Editor and Executive Marketing Manager, High School: Dan McDonough
Editorial Assistant: Amanda Legee
Production Assistant: Elise Keller
Copy Editor: Kathleen Benn McQueen
Text Permissions Manager: Kalina K. Ingham
Photo Permissions Manager: Martha Friedman
Senior Art Director: Anna Palchik
Text Design: Claire Seng-Niemoeller
Cover Design: Donna Lee Dennison
Cover Photos: All cover photos courtesy of Masterfile. Marathon Dolphin Sanctuary © Mark Downey; beach with palm trees © Dhoxax; flamingo © jonnysek; lone paddler at sunset, Siesta Key Beach © erichinson; young woman snorkeling © GoodOlga; Miami skyline © badboo.
Project Management and Composition: Books By Design, Inc.
Printing and Binding: RR Donnelley and Sons

President, Bedford/St. Martin's: Denise B. Wydra
Presidents, Macmillan Higher Education: Joan E. Feinberg and Tom Scotty
Editor in Chief: Karen S. Henry
Director of Marketing: Karen R. Soeltz
Production Director: Susan W. Brown
Associate Production Director: Elise S. Kaiser
Managing Editor: Elizabeth M. Schaaf

Manufactured in the United States of America.

7 6 5 4 3 2
f e d c b a

For information, write: Bedford/St. Martin's, 75 Arlington Street, Boston, MA 02116
(617-399-4000)

ISBN: 978-1-4576-4202-9

Acknowledgments

Acknowledgments and copyrights are continued at the back of the book on pages 155–56, which constitute an extension of the copyright page. It is a violation of the law to reproduce these selections by any means whatsoever without the written permission of the copyright holder.

Contents

Florida: A General Introduction   5

A Collection of Florida Literature   11

Illustrations

FLORIDA LITERATURE
A Case Study

Introduction to This Collection

CAROLINA HOSPITAL

Carolina Hospital is a poet, an essayist, and a novelist who teaches at Miami Dade College, where she has been awarded two endowed teaching chairs, in 1996 and in 2003. Her most recent publication, *The Child of Exile: A Poetry Memoir*, was published by Arte Publico Press of the University of Houston. Her short fiction, essays, and poems have appeared in numerous national magazines, newspapers, and anthologies, including *The Norton Anthology of Latino Literature*, *Prairie Schooner*, the *Washington Post*, the *Miami Herald*, *Wachale!: Poetry and Prose about Growing Up Latino*, and *Cool Salsa*. To date, she has published five books, including the novel *A Little Love*, under the pen name C. C. Medina, and *A Century of Cuban Writers in Florida*, a seminal work for understanding the cultural history of Florida. She also participated with thirteen South Florida authors, including Carl Hiaasen, James Hall, Dave Barry, and Edna Buchanan, in the *New York Times*'s best-selling novel *Naked Came the Manatee*.

Courtesy of Carlos Medina.

Sorting Florida

"As you drive North, you travel South," we often joke in Miami. Actually, while South Florida, especially Miami and the Keys, feels closer to the Caribbean than to the rest of the United States, in many ways North Florida resembles Georgia or Alabama. It has much to do with the landscape but also with the history, the population, even the political and social attitudes. In fact, Florida's identity is as elusive as the coastal sawfish described in Jack Rudloe's essay in this anthology. And the writers you will read in this book—writers who define this identity through their imaginations—share in shaping it.

Florida is both illusion and reality. And that reality is as much a product of the imagination as the result of a series of historical events or a mound of limestone. Wallace Stevens suggests as much in "The Idea of Order at Key West": "And when she sang, the sea / Whatever self it had, became the self / That was her song, for she was the maker." Many writers, from the recorders of early folksongs and tales to contemporary urban authors, have attempted to depict this complex place, to give it song, and in doing so have contributed to its understanding and characterization. For my part, I would choose one word to convey Florida: *paradox*.

From its inception, this peninsula served as both subjugation and sanctuary. Spaniards arrived in Florida in the early 1500s, seeking riches and a fabled fountain of youth, giving the state its name because they landed probably near St. Augustine on Easter Sunday, "Pascua Florida." The conquerors confronted various indigenous tribes such as the Calusa in the southwest, the Tequesta in the southeast, the Timucua in the center and northeast, and the Apalachee in the northwest. Despite resistance, to a certain measure, the Spaniards succeeded in colonizing and Christianizing Florida.

In the early colonial period, Florida's economic dependence on Cuba was almost complete, due in part to Florida's lack of resources and in part to Cuba's proximity, which facilitated most of the peninsula's trade and commerce. During this time, Florida was governed from Havana, reinforcing a link that would stretch throughout the centuries. Except for a brief period of British occupation, Florida remained under Spanish domination until 1821.

Paradoxically, Florida became a sanctuary for runaway slaves from neighboring states who often lived among the subjugated native tribes. In great part, their presence provoked Andrew Jackson's military incursions into Florida to force the relocation of slaves and the removal of the Seminoles. Today, reservations occupied by Florida's native people exist at Immokalee, Hollywood, Brighton (near the city of Okeechobee), and along the Big Cypress Swamp. In addition to the Seminole people, South Florida harbors a separate Miccosukee tribe, the subject of "Say These Names (Remember Them)" by Betty Sue Cummings.

By the end of the nineteenth century, however, Florida was offering sanctuary to Cuban refugees, first to those escaping the devastation of the Cuban Wars of Independence from Spain and much later because of dictator Fidel Castro's takeover of Cuba. The bonds with Cuba created during the Spanish colonial period have been renewed time and time again. The lure of this Caribbean island so close to Florida's shore fascinated many, including writers such as Stephen Crane, who served as a war correspondent in Cuba during the Spanish-American War; Ernest Hemingway, who eventually moved there from Key West; and, more recently, Jimmy Buffett.

For most of the nineteenth century and early twentieth century, Key West served as a safe haven for an eclectic group: North American writers, such as Hemingway, Elizabeth Bishop, and Tennessee Williams, enticed by this tiny key's tropical, diverse, and unfettered ambience; bootleggers trying to avoid Prohibition; U.S. military personnel stationed on land and at sea during multiple wars; and the Cubans fleeing the war-torn island, such as Diego Vicente Tejera. (By 1959, Miami had replaced Key West as a destination for Cuban exiles.) For many of the writers in Key West, and throughout all of Florida, living in a landscape lapped by water, the sea held a seductive appeal, almost as if the Gulf Stream were the last American frontier.

Most Florida literary works feel distinctly embedded in either sea or soil. While many of the readings in the anthology recount mishaps at sea—rip currents and undertows, shoals and bights, gulf weed and low tides, cold waters and distant shores—others, especially as we travel further north, repeatedly contain imagery of pine woods, oak hammocks, cypress swamps, riverbanks, and Spanish moss. A keen eye that captures, even defends, the state's natural character, defines Florida literature. Whether it's an essay directly advocating the protection of the environment or a story about a boy and his fawn or a man and his sawfish, nature takes on a central and distinctive quality. These texts helped shape the Eden-like vision of the state while sounding a warning bell. Florida's population has dramatically grown since the last half of the twentieth century: the thirty-second most populous state in 1900 jumped to fourth place by 1990. This increase has had grievous consequences for the natural environment while simultaneously encouraging the conservation of this Florida "paradise."

As beaches and scrublands are juxtaposed, so is an Old World nostalgic vision pitted against a New World city view. In Florida, the long familiar lives alongside the new and the foreign. The rural stands out against the urban. Contradictions coexist here. It's what both enriches and frustrates Floridians. Longtime residents have to navigate alongside newcomers: retiring snowbirds from northern states, transplants following executive jobs or college programs, immigrants from mostly the Caribbean and Latin America. Each group's goal or perception of what community is may differ greatly.

Florida has been shaped by these contradictions for centuries. Writers have been drawn to them and challenged by them, eager to chronicle and dissect them. Dave Barry relishes satirizing the Emerald City of Florida, Disney World, while Joan Didion confronts the cocaine cowboys' drug violence of the 1980s. Each writer connects a piece of the puzzle that makes up the state; as a whole, they begin to capture the complexity of its illusionary and real character. In 1873, Harriet Beecher Stowe points out that "full half of the tourists and travellers that come to Florida return intensely disappointed," their romantic notions bumping up against the reality of a complicated prickly state with "a general disarray and dazzle." This may have been true back then, but today the disarray and dazzle are part of Florida's attraction. As Elizabeth Bishop similarly writes half a century later, "All the untidy activity continues, awful but cheerful."

Can a place be awful but cheerful? For me, the answer is yes. I live these paradoxes every day. They define the state and contribute to its appeal. Florida is a multifaceted, challenging, and beautiful place, at once nostalgic and full of promise; mature and adolescent; grounding and eluding. It has a rich history and heritage as well as a priceless and varied environment; however, these are too often unfamiliar to its inhabitants. In order to care for a place, you have to first understand it.

Writers help us to care. They unravel what is complicated, define what is ignored, and depict what amuses or enthralls us. In doing so, they engage us. That engagement is the first step toward seeing the possibilities of a more inclusive future, for Florida and the entire country.

I hope this anthology will whet your appetite and encourage you to determine for yourself the true nature of this intriguing and captivating state. Indeed may these texts serve as Tennessee Williams's diving-bell, allowing you to "go under the sea" and "return to the surface with ominous wonders to tell" about Florida.

— C.H.

Florida: A General Introduction

Florida, 1845. This is an early map, after Florida became a state the same year. Shown here, referring to the Second Seminole War (1835–1842), are routes taken by the army.
Courtesy of Joseph H. Fitzgerald, Chairman of the Miami Map Fair.

ANNE E. ROWE

Anne E. Rowe (b. 1945) is the Dean of Faculties and Deputy Provost at Florida State University. She holds a Ph.D. in literature from the University of North Carolina at Chapel Hill and has published two books of literary criticism, *The Enchanted Country: Northern Writers in the South, 1865–1910* (1978) and *The Idea of Florida in the American Literary Imagination* (1986), from which this essay is excerpted. She is currently writing a book that analyzes domestic imagery used by southern women writers, and she publishes articles and essays on southern literature in numerous journals, including the *Encyclopedia of Southern Culture*.

Courtesy of Anne E. Rowe.

BEFORE YOU READ

In the following essay, Rowe outlines the appeal of both the "real" and the "imaginative" Florida. As you read, think about how these aspects of the state are differentiated. How also are they perhaps equally important, according to Rowe?

On the Idea of Florida in the American Literary Imagination 1986

In the half-century since Wallace Stevens made Florida a part of his dialectic between reality and the imagination, Florida has continued to be important both as a real part of the nation and as a source of imaginative appeal. World War II affected Florida much the same way as had the wars preceding it, though on a larger scale. Again thousands of servicemen were sent to Florida for training, and many of them would return to Florida to live after the war ended. Although the war initially had an adverse effect on tourism in Florida, more than five hundred resort hotels were leased by the government for military uses, thus salvaging the state's economy. The Ponce de León, for example, became for a while a Coast Guard indoctrination center. After 1943 tourism again was in full swing, and the economy was also boosted by industrial military installations, especially shipyards. Florida's population has continued to swell from an influx of people seeking what has been called the best winter climate in the United States. The 1950s saw Florida developing from a rural-dominated state to an urban one. Between 1950 and 1983 Florida grew from the twentieth to the seventh largest state in the nation, and still the people come. Perhaps in no other state have the conflicting goals of growth and preservation from destruction of the very natural resources that have attracted people been so apparent as they are in Florida.

At the same time that Florida (in spite of the threat to the state's ecology) has gained an increasingly important place in the economy and technology of the nation, its continued imaginative appeal is much in evidence. Somehow it is not surprising that Florida has played such an important role in space exploration, that it is from Florida that each new American rocket is launched. And it is also in Florida that the largest embodiments of fantasy and technology—Disney World and Epcot—have been created out of the very swamps and barrens of Florida that Henry James despaired of, suggesting that even if Florida the real is finally lost a man-made paradise will take its place.

Although Florida has continued to evoke a literary response—Elizabeth Bishop, Jesse Hill Ford, Harry Crews, among others, have treated Florida in their work—it seems in some ways appropriate that Florida has become even more prominent in the film medium, as in movies like *Midnight Cowboy*. Two hundred years after Bartram succumbed to a vision of this place, the idea of Florida still evokes an imaginative response. The land of Florida remains an enchanted country—a place seductively different from the ordinary, a land where dreams just might come true.

QUESTIONS FOR CRITICAL THINKING AND WRITING

1. In paragraph 1, Rowe states, "Perhaps in no other state have the conflicting goals of growth and preservation from destruction of the very natural resources that have attracted people been so apparent as they are in Florida." How does she illustrate these conflicting goals, and why do these conflicting goals exist?

2. This essay was published in 1986. How has "Florida the real" changed since then? Do you believe that Rowe's overarching ideas about the state remain true? Why or why not?

3. Are there other states in this country that face a dilemma like Florida, in terms of the natural versus "man-made"? What are they, and what are the similarities between those states? What are the differences?

A Collection
of Florida Literature

DAVE BARRY

Dave Barry (b. 1947) is an American author whose syndicated humor columns ran in national newspapers for twenty-five years. The author of more than thirty books and collections, Barry retired from writing his regular column in 2004. He still writes occasional articles and published the book *I'll Mature When I'm Dead* in 2010. In an article in the Haverford alumni magazine, Barry joked that he started his career in newspaper "because [he] was an English major" and

Courtesy of Larry Marano/Getty Images.

therefore "had plenty of experience writing long, authoritative-sounding essays without any knowledge of [his] topic, which is of course the essence of journalism."

BEFORE YOU READ

Dave Barry's "The Walt 'You Will Have Fun' Disney World Themed Shopping Complex and Resort Compound" is a satirical examination of Disney World. As you read, identify where you can tell that Barry is using satire — what words, phrases, or punctuation clearly illustrate that he is not being sincere?

The Walt "You Will Have Fun" Disney World Themed Shopping Complex and Resort Compound   *1991*

I'm an expert on visiting Disney World, because we live only four hours away, and according to my records we spend about three-fifths of our after-tax income there. Not that I'm complaining. You can't have a bad time at Disney World. It's not *allowed*. They have hidden electronic surveillance cameras everywhere, and if they catch you failing to laugh with childlike wonder, they lock you inside a costume representing a beloved Disney character such as Goofy and make you walk around in the Florida heat getting grabbed and leaped on by violently excited children until you have learned your lesson. Yes, Disney World is a "dream vacation," and here are some tips to help make it "come true" for you!

When to Go: The best time to go, if you want to avoid huge crowds, is 1962.

How to Get There: It's possible to fly, but if you want the total Disney World experience, you should drive there with a minimum of four hostile children via the longest possible route. If you live in Georgia, for example, you should plan a route that includes Oklahoma.

Once you get to Florida, you can't miss Disney World, because the Disney corporation owns the entire center of the state. Just get on any major highway, and eventually it will dead-end in a Disney parking area large enough to have its own climate, populated by large nomadic families who have been trying to find their cars since the Carter administration. Be sure to note carefully where you leave *your* car, because later on you may want to sell it so you can pay for your admission tickets.

But never mind the price; the point is that now you're finally *there*, in the ultimate vacation fantasy paradise, ready to have fun! Well, okay, you're not exactly there *yet*. First you have to wait for the parking-lot tram, driven by cheerful uniformed Disney employees, to come around and pick you up and give you a helpful lecture about basic tram-safety rules such as never fall out of the tram without coming to a full and complete stop.

But now the tram ride is over and it's time for fun! Right? Don't be an idiot. It's time to wait in line to buy admission tickets. Most experts recommend that you go with the 47-day pass, which will give you a chance, if you never eat or sleep, to visit *all* of the Disney themed attractions, including The City of the Future, The Land of Yesterday, The Dull Suburban Residential Community of Sometime Next Month, Wet Adventure, Farms on Mars, The World of Furniture, Sponge Encounter, the Nuclear Flute Orchestra, Appliance Island, and the Great Underwater Robot Hairdresser Adventure, to name just a few.

Okay, you've taken out a second mortgage and purchased your tickets! Now, finally, it's time to . . . wait in line again! This time, it's for the monorail, a modern, futuristic transportation system that whisks you to the Magic Kingdom at nearly half the speed of a lawn tractor. Along the way cheerful uniformed Disney World employees will offer you some helpful monorail-safety tips such as never set fire to the monorail without first removing your personal belongings.

And now, at last, you're at the entrance to the Magic Kingdom itself! No more waiting in line for transportation! It's time to *wait in line to get in*. Wow! Look at all the *other* people waiting to get in! There are tour groups here with names like "Entire Population of Indiana." There sure must be some great attractions inside these gates!

And now you've inched your way to the front of the line, and the cheerful uniformed Disney employee is stamping your hand with a special invisible chemical that penetrates your nervous system and causes you to temporarily acquire the personality of a cow. "Moo!" you shout as you surge forward with the rest of the herd.

And now, unbelievably, you're actually inside the Magic Kingdom! At last! Mecca! You crane your head to see over the crowd around you, and with innocent childlike wonder you behold: *a much larger crowd*. Ha ha! You are having some kind of fun now!

And now you are pushing your way forward, thrusting other vacationers aside, knocking over their strollers if necessary, because little Jason wants to ride on Space Mountain. Little Jason has been talking about Space Mountain ever since Oklahoma, and by God you're going to take him on it, no matter how long the . . . My God! Can *this* be the line for Space Mountain? This line is so long that there are Cro-Magnon families at the front! Perhaps if you explain to little Jason that he could be a deceased old man by the time he gets on the actual ride, he'll agree to skip it and . . . NO! Don't scream, little Jason! We'll just purchase some official Mickey Mouse sleeping bags, and we'll stay in line as long as it takes! The hell with third grade! We'll just stand here and chew our cuds! Mooooo!

Speaking of education, you should be sure to visit Epcot Center, which features exhibits sponsored by large corporations showing you how various challenges facing the human race are being met and overcome thanks to the

1,500 Disney employees in front of Cinderella Castle

LIFE

Disney World Opens

OCTOBER 15 • 1971 • 50¢

Life, **October 15, 1971, Disney World Opens.** *Life* magazine, which ran from 1936 to 2000, is known for capturing some of the most iconic moments of the twentieth century. Here, the opening of Disney World in 1971 made the front cover.

Yale Joel/Time & Life Pictures/Getty Images.

selfless efforts of large corporations. Epcot Center also features pavilions built by various foreign nations, where you can experience an extremely realistic simulation of what life in these nations would be like if they consisted almost entirely of restaurants and souvenir shops.

One memorable Epcot night my family and I ate at the German restaurant, where I had several large beers and a traditional German delicacy called "Bloatwurst," which is a sausage that can either be eaten or used as a tackling dummy. When we got out I felt like one of those snakes that eat a cow whole and then just lie around and digest it for a couple of months. But my son was determined to go on a new educational Epcot ride called "The Body," wherein you sit in a compartment that simulates what it would be like if you got inside a spaceship-like vehicle and got shrunk down to the size of a gnat and got injected inside a person's body.

I'll tell you what it's like: awful. You're looking at a screen showing an extremely vivid animated simulation of the human interior, which is not the most appealing way to look at a human unless you're attracted to white blood cells the size of motor homes. Meanwhile the entire compartment is bouncing you around violently, especially when you go through the aorta. "Never go through the aorta after eating German food," that is my new travel motto.

What gets me is, I waited in line for an *hour* to do this. I could have experienced essentially the same level of enjoyment merely by sticking my finger down my throat.

Which brings me to my idea for getting rich. No doubt you have noted that, in most amusement parks, the popularity of a ride is directly proportional to how horrible it is. There's hardly ever a line for nice, relaxing rides like the merry-go-round. But there will always be a huge crowd, mainly consisting of teenagers, waiting to go on a ride with a name like "The Dicer," where they strap people into what is essentially a giant food processor and turn it on and then phone the paramedics.

So my idea is to open up a theme park called "Dave World," which will have a ride called "The Fall of Death." This will basically be a 250-foot tower. The way it will work is, you climb to the top, a trapdoor opens up, and you splat onto the asphalt below like a bushel of late-summer tomatoes.

Obviously, for legal reasons, I couldn't let anybody actually *go* on this ride. There would be a big sign that said:

WARNING!
NOBODY CAN GO ON THIS RIDE.
THIS RIDE IS INVARIABLY FATAL.
THANK YOU.

But this would only make The Fall of Death more popular. Every teenager in the immediate state would come to Dave World just to stand in line for it.

Dave World would also have an attraction called "Parentland," which would have a sign outside that said: "Sorry, Kids! This Attraction Is for Mom 'n' Dad Only!" Inside would be a bar. For younger children, there would be "Soil Fantasy," a themed play area consisting of dirt or, as a special "rainy-day" bonus, mud.

I frankly can't see how Dave World could fail to become a huge financial success that would make me rich and enable me to spend the rest of my days traveling the world with my family. So the hell with it.

Seeing Other Attractions in the Disney World Area

You must be very careful here. You must sneak out of Disney World in the dead of night, because the Disney people do *not* want you leaving the compound and spending money elsewhere. If they discover that you're gone, cheerful uniformed employees led by Mickey Mouse's lovable dog Pluto, who will sniff the ground in a comical manner, will track you down. And when they catch you, it's *into the Goofy suit.*

So we're talking about a major risk, but it's worth it for some of the attractions around Disney World. The two best ones, as it happens, are right next to each other near a town called Kissimmee. One of them is the world headquarters of the Tupperware company, where you can take a guided tour that includes a Historic Food Containers Museum. I am not making this up.

I am also not making up Gatorland, which is next door. After entering Gatorland through a giant pair of pretend alligator jaws, you find yourself on walkways over a series of murky pools in which are floating a large number of alligators that appear to be recovering from severe hangovers, in the sense that they hardly ever move. You can purchase fish to feed them, but the typical Gatorland alligator will ignore a fish even if it lands directly on its head. Sometimes you'll see an alligator, looking bored, wearing three or four rotting, fly-encrusted fish, like some kind of High Swamp Fashion headgear.

This is very entertaining, of course, but the *real* action at Gatorland, the event that brings even the alligators to life, is the Assault on the Dead Chickens, which is technically known as the Gator Jumparoo. I am also not making this up. The way it works is, a large crowd of tourists gathers around a central pool, over which, suspended from wires, are a number of plucked headless chicken carcasses. As the crowd, encouraged by the Gatorland announcer, cheers wildly, the alligators lunge out of the water and rip the chicken carcasses down with their jaws. Once you've witnessed this impressive event, you will never again wonder how America got to be the country that it is today.

QUESTIONS FOR CRITICAL THINKING AND WRITING

1. How does Barry describe Epcot Center? What are the attractions of that particular area of the park, and what does he think of them?

2. Barry gives readers plenty of reasons not to visit Disney World—price, crowds, lines, and so on—but he himself still goes, and it is still wildly popular. What are some of the fun or entertaining aspects of Disney World that Barry does not mention here? Why do you think he avoids mentioning them? How do these omissions serve the overall purpose of his essay?

3. Barry closes his essay with a statement about "how America got to be the country that it is today." What is he saying about America here? Is it a positive or negative statement? How so?

Disney's influence doesn't end with its theme park. The company has made its mark in Florida in countless ways, producing many television shows and films at their studios—and set, quite often affectionately, in the state.

Flight of the Navigator, 1986. Set and filmed in Fort Lauderdale, this Disney science fiction film relies on its setting—making the state something of a character in the movie as well.
Flight of the Navigator, Joey Cramer, 1986, © Buena Vista Pictures/Courtesy Everett Collection.

The Golden Girls, which ran on NBC from 1985 to 1992, also treated Florida—and especially Miami—as a character. Exterior shots of the iconic house where Dorothy, Blanche, Rose, and Sophia live were filmed at Disney-MGM studios. For many years, it was a featured part of the tour through the studios' "Residential Street."
NBC/Getty Images.

Their Eyes Were Watching God, 2005. Zora Neale Hurston is one of Florida's most beloved writers, and her 1937 novel, *Their Eyes Were Watching God,* is her most renowned book. Oprah Winfrey and ABC, which is owned by Disney, were responsible for bringing this film adaptation, starring Halle Berry, to the small screen.
Photofest, Inc.

Cougar Town, an ABC-produced show that premiered in 2009, also takes its setting—the fictional town of Gulfhaven, Florida—and proudly showcases it front and center, this time with a twenty-first-century makeover.
Photofest, Inc.

ELIZABETH BISHOP

Elizabeth Bishop was born in Worcester, Massachusetts, in 1911. When she was a young child, her father died and her mother was institutionalized, so she was sent to live with her grandparents. She attended Vassar College from 1929 to 1934, where she began to hone her writing skills and was introduced to the poetry of Marianne Moore, who would become her most important influence. Bishop was the recipient of the Pulitzer Prize in 1956, and she won the National Book Award in 1969. She died in 1979.

Courtesy of Bettmann/Corbis.

BEFORE YOU READ

Elizabeth Bishop is known for her ability to craft extraordinary imagery in her poetry. As you read "The Bight," take note of the different images Bishop uses. How do these images create a scene, and what emotion does that scene then evoke?

The Bight   *1983*
[On my Birthday]

At low tide like this how sheer the water is.
White, crumbling ribs of marl protrude and glare
and the boats are dry, the pilings dry as matches.
Absorbing, rather than being absorbed,
the water in the bight doesn't wet anything,   5
the color of the gas flame turned as low as possible.
One can smell it turning to gas; if one were Baudelaire
one could probably hear it turning to marimba music.
The little ocher dredge at work off the end of the dock
already plays the dry perfectly off-beat claves.   10
The birds are outsize. Pelicans crash
into this peculiar gas unnecessarily hard,
it seems to me, like pickaxes,
rarely coming up with anything to show for it,
and going off with humorous elbowings.   15
Black-and-white man-of-war birds soar
on impalpable drafts
and open their tails like scissors on the curves
or tense them like wishbones, till they tremble.
The frowsy sponge boats keep coming in   20

with the obliging air of retrievers,
bristling with jackstraw gaffs and hooks
and decorated with bobbles of sponges.
There is a fence of chicken wire along the dock
where, glinting like little plowshares,   25
the blue-gray shark tails are hung up to dry
for the Chinese-restaurant trade.
Some of the little white boats are still piled up
against each other, or lie on their sides, stove in,
and not yet salvaged, if they ever will be, from the last bad storm,   30
like torn-open, unanswered letters.
The bight is littered with old correspondences.
Click. Click. Goes the dredge,
and brings up a dripping jawful of marl.
All the untidy activity continues,   35
awful but cheerful.

QUESTIONS FOR CRITICAL THINKING AND WRITING

1. "The Bight" consists mainly of images that paint a picture of the ocean at low tide, but the metaphors Bishop chooses to illustrate these images are suggestive of a deeper meaning. Choose at least two such metaphors and explain what they might mean on both an aesthetic and a symbolic level.

2. What might the subtitle, "[On my Birthday]," signal to the reader of the poem? Why do you think Bishop chose to include that subtitle in a seemingly impersonal poem?

3. In line 31, Bishop describes boats as "torn-open, unanswered letters" and says, "The bight is littered with old correspondences." What might Bishop mean by this simile, and how could it give insight into a more personal reading of the poem?

4. CONNECT TO ANOTHER READING. Both Elizabeth Bishop's "The Bight" and Wallace Stevens's "The Idea of Order at Key West" (p. 125) provide rich descriptions of the ocean. In a short essay, compare and contrast the way the ocean is portrayed in each poem, and the different meanings the ocean comes to symbolize in each poem.

The Armory, Key West. Elizabeth Bishop is best known as a writer, but she was also a prolific painter. This watercolor, gouache, and ink work depicts the Key West Armory on White Street, close to the home where Bishop lived from 1938 to 1941.

Courtesy of Farrar, Straus and Giroux.

JIMMY BUFFETT

Jimmy Buffett (b. 1946) is an American singer, songwriter, and author whose laid-back attitude and affinity for island living has spawned a devoted group of fans known as "Parrotheads." He splits his time between Palm Beach, Florida, and his house in St. Barth's. He is the author of several books, including *A Pirate Looks at Fifty*, which in 1998 took the number-one spot on the *New York Times* best-seller list.

Courtesy of Eddie Adams/Corbis.

BEFORE YOU READ

Cuba and Florida are culturally interwoven in many ways. Because of their proximity to each other and the established presence of Cuban Americans, southern Florida is heavily influenced by Cuban culture. Jimmy Buffett's "Hooked in the Heart" describes this connection and gives readers a glimpse into Cuba itself. What kinds of parallels does Buffett draw between Florida and Cuba? What similarities in Cuban and Floridian culture does he describe in this essay?

Hooked in the Heart   1989

To this day *The Old Man and the Sea* is one of my favorite books. I have read it at least a dozen times, and the characters are like close friends. You don't see them for long stretches of time, but when they suddenly appear again, it is as if they never left.

I still have my first copy of the book. Someone gave it to me for a Christmas or birthday present long ago, and it has traveled well because it is small. I first read it when I was eight years old. The relationship between the old man and the boy is what was most touching, because it reminded me so much of my grandfather and me.

Yesterday I had a pretty good day out bonefishing, exercising the "gray ghosts of the flats." There is an energy in these waters like nowhere else; the headwaters of the Gulf Stream squeeze between the land masses of Florida and Cuba, and the collision and overlapping of the Gulf of Mexico and the Caribbean Sea affects human and animal behavior in more ways than Heinz has sauces.

When I hung my fly rods back in their racks on the ceiling, I accidentally knocked a book from the shelf. The familiar faded blue book lay on the floor.

Instead of returning it to its place on the shelf, I mixed myself a rum drink, settled down in the Florida room, and opened the book to the first page.

A flock of roseate spoonbills landed gently in the salt pond across the canal to find their supper in the shallow water, and I worked my way comfortably into the couch with *The Old Man and the Sea*. I read the first chapter and the description of the old man in the village, and I looked at the photograph on the wall above me. It was a picture of Jane and me, taken with Gregorio Fuentes, the real-life "old man."

Several years ago I hooked up with a documentary film crew retracing Hemingway's hangouts with the help of his son and granddaughter. I threw in with them for a chance to go to Cuba.

When the Hollywood circus comes to town, I am always amazed to see how the chance to be on camera — or just make breakfast for the cast — completely transforms people. They will lie, cheat, steal, quit their jobs, commit acts of adultery, fall in love for the weekend, and sell their children into slavery just to say they are in the movies.

I was as much a victim of this plague as anyone. And when I was contacted about composing some music for the project, I agreed to forgo my usual fee for the chance to accompany this ship of fools aboard the old schooner *Western Union* on her ninety-mile crossing from Key West to Havana.

The whole time I had lived in Key West, Havana had intrigued me, especially the tales of the "old days" when the ferryboats made daily runs to the casinos and art deco hotels. Life here was much more connected to Cuba than to America.

Before that, my grandfather's sailing ships constantly called on Havana, and I had read many of his old logbook and journal entries. This added to my vision of the city. It had been the hub of activity when the Spanish first entered this hemisphere. My father had spent his first birthday on board a ship in Havana harbor, and when my grandfather raised all of his signal flags into the rigging to celebrate, so did every other sailing ship in the harbor.

We left Key West at midnight on the old schooner, sailing under a crescent moon. We arrived off the Cuban shore around noon the next day and were greeted by a pair of patrol boats manned by young boys shouldering AK-47s. Our stony faced escorts took us past the skyline of Havana and then into port.

We were driven by car down a boulevard that stretched for miles. It was lined with large, unoccupied houses. When we finally reached the city, we were taken to the Hotel Habana Libre. We checked in and found a microphone dangling from an air vent in the bathroom. I quickly composed a song entitled "Speak into the Shower Stall, Please" and sang it into the little condenser mike, wondering who was listening on the other end.

I wasn't due to work until that night, so Jane and I set out to look around and take in the sights, all two of them. The entire afternoon we were followed by secret police who seem to have watched too much "Yankee TV," to judge by the way they popped in and out of doorways and hid behind signs, tailing us to the Floridita restaurant. I waved and yelled for them to join us for lunch, but they quickly buried their faces in their newspapers and tried to look nonchalant.

We ordered daiquiris and stone crabs that came from the deep waters near the old Morro Castle. Then a trio sang "Guantanamera" in perfect harmony while we drank a bottle of Rumania's finest wine.

After lunch we took in the Museum of the Revolution, which is sort of like a little commie Disney World. The boat Fidel came ashore on sits in a bubble, and an old airplane hangs from a wire above. Cisco and Pancho were still hot on our trail. We meandered through Old Havana past the ancient cathedral, and I was reminded of some sections of Paris — except for the hundreds of vintage Chevys, Fords, Pontiacs, and DeSotos parked on the cobblestone streets.

That night I was to perform for the film in La Bodeguita del Medio, which was, in its day, one of the great bars of the world. In prerevolutionary days, Fidel, Salvador Allende, and Papa Hemingway were regulars. There they discussed the fate of the world over *mojitos*, a wonderful rum drink for which the bar was known. Now La Bodeguita del Medio attracts Canadian tourists and Russian workers on holiday.

The film crew was busy at work, and the place was packed with stony faced "customers" checking out the film crew at work. I finally spotted Cisco and Pancho in the corner and sent them a couple of drinks, but then it was lights, camera, and action time. There I was, singing "Havana Daydreamin'" to a bar full of cops who did not have a clue about who I was, what I was doing in Cuba, or what I was singing about. Nevertheless, they were wildly enthusiastic when I finished the song and bought us lots of *mojitos*. I love show business.

We stayed until closing time, but our Foreign Ministry guides left early, so we took a cab back to the hotel with Cisco and Pancho following us in a black '53 Ford. Driving through the dark, deserted streets of Old Havana, I felt as if I were in an old "Boston Blackie" episode.

Our cab driver was checking us out in the rearview mirror, and I'm sure it wasn't hard for him to figure out we weren't working for the government. He switched the tape from a Cuban salsa band to the Rolling Stones, double-shifted the car, and took the turn onto the main drag with his tires squealing. He flashed an excited smile at us, raised a clenched fist, and shouted, "Rock 'n' roll."

The next morning Peter, the producer of the film, called me much too early and asked if I wanted to go out with him to meet Gregorio Fuentes. He said he was waiting to get permission from the Foreign Ministry to go out early.

I had heard this old man was the inspiration for one of my favorite books, and I was not going to miss the opportunity to meet the man behind the myth. We gathered in the lobby and waited for the Foreign Ministry people to show. But after almost two hours, we took off without them. This gave Cisco and Pancho a morning workout they were not expecting.

We lost them at a downtown intersection when we changed taxis and soon were out of the busy city and on our way to Cojímar, where Gregorio lived.

The cab dropped us off at the entrance to the village, and it was like stepping into the first chapter of the book. We walked down sand streets past the old battery that guarded the harbor, and in the center of town we came upon a monument that had been erected to Hemingway.

Cojímar was still a fishing village. No tourist information booths, no beach rental stands, and this day we were the only gringos in town. It was very hot, and no breeze blew in from the ocean. We stopped for a couple of beers and got directions to the old man's place. We found him sitting on the porch of a small stucco house behind a bougainvillea hedge, smoking a cigar almost as big as he was. From the road, we introduced ourselves, and he motioned for us to join him on the veranda.

Peter was our interpreter and told the old man what we were doing there. The old man just seemed happy to have visitors and immediately launched into a fishing story, telling us of a fish he had caught last week. It had cut his hand badly. He raised his right hand and pointed to the fresh, deep cut, but it could barely be seen among the hundreds of other scar lines — an occupational hazard.

Although I could not understand Gregorio's words, I felt what he was communicating. The story of his life was in his eyes and his hands. He wanted to show us his new boat in the boatyard on the east end of the beach, so we walked over together, followed by young inquisitive faces that darted in and out of our path like hungry minnows. I asked the old man if Papa Hemingway had left him any mementos, thinking he might have a classic rod or reel or cherished photos. He took a long draw on the cigar, looked up at the sun, and patted his heart with his hand.

Walking beside him down the beach, I asked if he had ever seen the movie version of *The Old Man and the Sea*. He had, but he didn't seem too flattered by Spencer Tracy's portrayal. When we got to the far end, Gregorio showed us his boat. It was a small skiff painted the color of the sea, and his eyes lit up as he told us of encounters with marlin so big they dined on sailfish. He showed us the marks on the bow of the tiny boat where sharks had attacked, and again he looked at his hands and pointed to a scar — the mark of yet another adventure.

We sat in the shade of a mahogany tree, and he told us a story about the time they were making the movie version of the book. The original director was fired and replaced by someone from the studio in Hollywood. Gregorio and Papa were fishing in Argentina when Hemingway heard the news. He went on a rampage and told Gregorio they were going back to Cuba to shoot the new director.

They boarded the plane in Buenos Aires for Havana, Hemingway wearing two pistols and carrying a bottle of rum, which they finished quickly. Apparently news of their impending arrival and proposed intentions were enough to cause the studio's director to lose interest in the film, and by the time Gregorio and Papa were back in town, the original director was rehired and on the job. Gregorio said Papa looked around, and, finding everything to his satisfaction, they were on the next plane back to Buenos Aires and fishing for trout the following day.

A large party was waiting to greet us when we returned to the old man's house. Cisco and Pancho were across the street in sweat-drenched suits, and our escorts from the Foreign Ministry very politely informed us that we were not to go anywhere without them in the future. We made our apologies, and then the old man said something to the young bureaucrats. They looked like children who had just been given a good scolding.

The film crew began to unload, and Cojímar buzzed with the preparations for the next day's shoot. I was so glad we had been able to share that little piece of time with the old man. He seemed absolutely content with his life as a fisherman.

God had given him the talent to bring to the surface fish larger even than the boat he used to pursue them. He didn't reject the fame and notoriety, but they were just secondary — spin-offs of his true talent. He was a model for growing old gracefully. His boat was his country, and he was the undisputed king. The political Cuisinart whirring away on dry land was of no concern to him.

The *Western Union* rounded the fort and entered the harbor with all her sails flying. We walked down to the pier where she would be docking. The town came alive with the arrival of the ship, and it was like being in another time. We boarded the boat, and Gregorio puffed away on his cigar, his eyes glued to the women in the crew; they scurried around the deck in bikinis. He looked over to the town square at a big crowd of excited teenage boys rattling on in Spanish, and he started to laugh. Peter asked what was happening, and Gregorio pointed to the women on deck and then to the boys on shore. "All those young boys are wondering why I am down here with all the pretty girls."

I noticed Cisco and Pancho perched up in a gumbo-limbo tree with their binoculars trained down on us, and I waved.

We were skimming the waves in my seaplane on our way out of Cuba, and flying fish as big as the plane leaped out of the water and swam in formation with us. I had jet engines now and was moving amazingly fast when I saw a small boat at twelve o'clock.

I descended gently into the ocean, and there was Gregorio, sitting in his little blue skiff, holding a handline and eating a mango. He invited me aboard for breakfast.

Suddenly one of the giant flying fish grabbed the line and started pulling the boat. We were off on a Nantucket sleigh ride. I panicked. My airplane was drifting away, and I was about to jump out of Gregorio's boat when he warned me that huge sharks surrounded us. I would be eaten alive. He pointed to the giant teeth embedded in the transom of his boat.

Next I knew, the fish was pulling us past Sand Key Light, and I saw Key West in the distance. A pink Coast Guard plane circled overhead. I said my good-byes to Gregorio and swam for the distant shore.

The airplane noise now sounded more like a mosquito in my ear, and I slapped at it and woke myself up. There was a little smear of blood and mangled wings; I had scored a direct hit. My copy of *The Old Man and the Sea* lay open across my chest, and crickets in the night-blooming jasmine began their symphony.

I walked outside with the dream still in my head and stared up at the clear sky, marveling at the fact that I lived on a little plug of dirt in the middle of two great oceans. I thought about Gregorio and wondered if he might be staring at the same stars from the other side of the Gulf Stream.

QUESTIONS FOR CRITICAL THINKING AND WRITING

1. Why does Buffett relate to Hemingway's novella *The Old Man and the Sea*? What are his personal connections to the book?

2. Who are Cisco and Pancho? Why does Buffett include them in the story, and what aspect of Cuba might they represent?

3. Why does Buffett relate the dream that he has about Gregorio? What is the significance of the dream, and what does it symbolize for Buffett?

4. **CONNECT TO ANOTHER READING.** Using the poems "How the Cubans Stole Miami" by Carolina Hospital (p. 77) and "For All the Goodbyes" by Silvia Curbelo (p. 52), and the story "Hooked in the Heart" by Jimmy Buffett, write a short essay in which you reflect on the representation of Cuba and Cubans in Floridian literature. How is the country portrayed? How are Cuban Americans portrayed? Can you draw any conclusions from these three texts about the relationship between Cuba and Florida? What are they?

SUSAN CERULEAN

Susan Cerulean is a Floridian writer and naturalist, and she is the director of the Red Hills Writers Project, a group of writers who live in the Red Hills and Gulf Coastal Lowland of Florida. Her most recent publication is a nature memoir titled *Tracking Desire: A Journey After Swallow-tailed Kites*. In 1997, Cerulean received the Individual Environmental Educator award from the Governor's Council for a Sustainable Florida.

BEFORE YOU READ

"'Restorying' Florida" is an essay about how to cultivate a permanent, identifiable vision of Florida. As many authors in this book have noted, a large number of residents of Florida are transient or temporary. In your opinion, does this affect the character of the state positively or negatively, or is this fact simply part of the character of the state as much as anything else? Explain your answer.

"Restorying" Florida 1999

Without stories, we do not know who we are, nor what we might become.
— D. H. Lawrence

The word "restoration" implies refilling, curing, setting right, caring for what has been injured. There are many hopeful examples of such landscape healings throughout Florida at present, from the Keys to the Ocklawaha River, from Tate's Hell Swamp to the Everglades. But it seems to me that even more will be required, beyond the considerable challenges of eliminating exotic plants, restoring natural flooding, and bringing back summer fire, if we are to truly heal all that ails our state.

That which we have overlooked is a "restorying" of the human inhabitants of Florida. Our population of 14 million is remarkably transient and overwhelmingly unfamiliar with our landscapes. Al Burt has written eloquently about the "absentee hearts" of many Floridians, whose bodies and winter homes are currently lodged in our state, but whose loyalties, and hearts, reside elsewhere.

It has not always been so.

The first humans arrived in Florida toward the end of the Pleistocene epoch, about 12,000 years ago, when much of North America was still covered with glaciers. Enormously complex and resilient native societies lived on this peninsula, fishing, collecting shellfish, hunting, gathering wild plants, and sometimes cultivating crops. Innumerable middens and mounds offer silent testimony to the Calusa, the Apalachee, the Tequesta, the Timucuan, the Hobe, the Matecumbe, the Tobago, and many others. They were threaded into their landscape like the palm fiber they wove into rope, and they knew well the plants and animals with whom they shared space, and had a name for each, and a story.

The root of our inability to imagine and create a hopeful, inclusive vision for Florida probably lies in the waves of European conquistadors who invaded Florida between 1500 and 1800 A.D., exterminating or driving out all our native inhabitants. With the genocide of the original peoples, we lost a profound opportunity to understand our landscape.

Why are the old stories that sprang from intimate contact with land so important to our present ecological dilemmas? Embedded in them is an old, old knowledge of how animals, including the human animal, can interact and cooperate with one another in a sustainable fashion. A shared oral or written tradition explains to us the land and its creatures and how they all relate. This context may be what keeps people home, tending the land and their lives within it.

However, in Florida, such a body of knowledge, accrued through 14,000 years of living in harmony on the land, has been superseded by 400 years of raid and pillage, greed, and an unengaged sort of tourism. These relatively new relationships to Florida are still the dominant paradigm today. The motives for coming to Florida, for most, have not included an interest in the fullness of what we are here. Florida State University religion professor Leo Sandon speaks of the two primary opportunities with which Florida has been identified through the years: a legitimized opportunity to raid and pillage, and an invitation to experience a tropical Eden.

The problem with both visions of Florida is that they do little to establish a sense of Florida as home. The first focuses on our ownership and development of the state, rather than on identification or kinship with it. The second dreams of this land as an enchanting but temporary place, a diversion from real life, a location where we might enjoy either our vacation or our retirement.

What does it mean to live on unstoried land? How does such poverty of heritage relate to attachment and stewardship of a landscape? Without a story, without specifying the sacred, we can hold nothing holy, or whole. We desecrate, we drain, ditch and dike, because "we know not what we do." Nor where we really are, nor what makes this place work.

What we need in Florida today, in theologian John Cobb's words, are new stories that "serve wellness, that move us towards a new narrative of restoration and hope, that recognize terrestrial intelligence."

I have a strong hunch that the real stories of Florida are so powerful, so gripping, so various, and so enriching that if we were to somehow reclaim them and weave them into our culture, things would be very different in our state. The notion of security as we view it now would seem gray and dull, compared to the life in the living forests and springs and prairies.

Despite our impoverished cultural legacy, there is a clearly marked signpost back to our true heritage in this landscape. The landscape itself, despite its tragic losses, remains storied, reminds the Chickasaw poet Linda Hogan. Florida's many restoration projects and its conserved wild places offer physical and spiritual maps to us. Here is how to read them.

Lie with your ear to the ground. Let birdsong trace its complexities onto your eardrum. Walk with your face in the wind, and dive into the cold waters. Listen with your heart.

Tell that story.

QUESTIONS FOR CRITICAL THINKING AND WRITING

1. According to Cerulean, what are the primary problems with the current population of Florida, and what effect can today's inhabitants have on the environment and the stories of the land?

2. What is Cerulean's argument regarding the importance of a storied land? What does she think will result from the current state of unstoried land?

3. In her essay, Cerulean refers to Florida's "impoverished cultural legacy." What does she mean by that phrase?

STEPHEN CRANE

Stephen Crane (1871–1900) was an American writer who is probably best known for his novel *The Red Badge of Courage* (1895). He was also a writer of short stories, though, and the following story, "The Open Boat," was based on his own experience of being stranded in a boat in the Atlantic Ocean. En route to Cuba to work as a war correspondent, Crane's ship sank, and he spent thirty hours in a dinghy with three other crew members before they washed ashore.

Courtesy of Kean Collection/Getty Images.

BEFORE YOU READ

Crane's "The Open Boat" is typically read as an existential story, in which humans are seen as insignificant in the grand scheme of the universe. As you read, ask yourself how this hopelessness is portrayed in the text, and what might be the motivation behind it.

The Open Boat   *1898*

I

None of them knew the color of the sky. Their eyes glanced level, and were fastened upon the waves that swept toward them. These waves were of the hue of slate, save for the tops, which were of foaming white, and all of the men knew the colors of the sea. The horizon narrowed and widened, and dipped and rose, and at all times its edge was jagged with waves that seemed thrust up in points like rocks. Many a man ought to have a bath-tub larger than the boat which here rode upon the sea. These waves were most wrongfully and barbarously abrupt and tall, and each froth-top was a problem in small boat navigation.

The cook squatted in the bottom and looked with both eyes at the six inches of gunwale which separated him from the ocean. His sleeves were rolled over his fat forearms, and the two flaps of his unbuttoned vest dangled as he bent to bail out the boat. Often he said: "Gawd! That was a narrow clip." As he remarked it he invariably gazed eastward over the broken sea.

The oiler, steering with one of the two oars in the boat, sometimes raised himself suddenly to keep clear of water that swirled in over the stern. It was a thin little oar and it seemed often ready to snap.

The correspondent, pulling at the other oar, watched the waves and wondered why he was there.

The injured captain, lying in the bow, was at this time buried in that profound dejection and indifference which comes, temporarily at least, to even the bravest and most enduring when, willy nilly, the firm fails, the army loses, the ship goes down. The mind of the master of a vessel is rooted deep in the timbers of her, though he command for a day or a decade, and this captain had on him the stern impression of a scene in the grays of dawn of seven turned faces, and later a stump of a top-mast with a white ball on it that slashed to and fro at the waves, went low and lower, and down.

Thereafter there was something strange in his voice. Although steady, it was deep with mourning, and of a quality beyond oration or tears.

"Keep'er a little more south, Billie," said he.

"'A little more south,' sir," said the oiler in the stern.

A seat in this boat was not unlike a seat upon a bucking broncho, and, by the same token, a broncho is not much smaller. The craft pranced and reared, and plunged like an animal. As each wave came, and she rose for it, she seemed like a horse making at a fence outrageously high. The manner of her scramble over these walls of water is a mystic thing, and, moreover, at the top of them were ordinarily these problems in white water, the foam racing down from the summit of each wave, requiring a new leap, and a leap from the air. Then, after scornfully bumping a crest, she would slide, and race, and splash down a long incline and arrive bobbing and nodding in front of the next menace.

A singular disadvantage of the sea lies in the fact that after successfully surmounting one wave you discover that there is another behind it just as important and just as nervously anxious to do something effective in the way of swamping boats. In a ten-foot dingey one can get an idea of the resources of the sea in the line of waves that is not probable to the average experience, which is never at sea in a dingey. As each slaty wall of water approached, it shut all else from the view of the men in the boat, and it was not difficult to imagine that this particular wave was the final outburst of the ocean, the last effort of the grim water. There was a terrible grace in the move of the waves, and they came in silence, save for the snarling of the crests.

In the wan light, the faces of the men must have been gray. Their eyes must have glinted in strange ways as they gazed steadily astern. Viewed from a balcony, the whole thing would doubtlessly have been weirdly picturesque. But the men in the boat had no time to see it, and if they had had leisure there were other things to occupy their minds. The sun swung steadily up the sky, and they knew it was broad day because the color of the sea changed from slate to emerald-green, streaked with amber lights, and the foam was like tumbling snow. The process of the breaking day was unknown to them. They were aware only of this effect upon the color of the waves that rolled toward them.

In disjointed sentences the cook and the correspondent argued as to the difference between a life-saving station and a house of refuge. The cook had said: "There's a house of refuge just north of the Mosquito Inlet Light, and as soon as they see us, they'll come off in their boat and pick us up."

"As soon as who see us?" said the correspondent.

"The crew," said the cook.

"Houses of refuge don't have crews," said the correspondent. "As I understand them, they are only places where clothes and grub are stored for the benefit of shipwrecked people. They don't carry crews."

"Oh, yes, they do," said the cook.

"No, they don't," said the correspondent.

"Well, we're not there yet, anyhow," said the oiler, in the stern.

"Well," said the cook, "perhaps it's not a house of refuge that I'm thinking of as being near Mosquito Inlet Light. Perhaps it's a life-saving station."

"We're not there yet," said the oiler, in the stern.

II

As the boat bounced from the top of each wave, the wind tore through the hair of the hatless men, and as the craft plopped her stern down again the spray slashed past them. The crest of each of these waves was a hill, from the top of which the men surveyed, for a moment, a broad tumultuous expanse; shining and wind-riven. It was probably splendid. It was probably glorious, this play of the free sea, wild with lights of emerald and white and amber.

"Bully good thing it's an on-shore wind," said the cook. "If not, where would we be? Wouldn't have a show."

"That's right," said the correspondent.

The busy oiler nodded his assent.

Then the captain, in the bow, chuckled in a way that expressed humor, contempt, tragedy, all in one. "Do you think we've got much of a show, now, boys?" said he.

Whereupon the three were silent, save for a trifle of hemming and hawing. To express any particular optimism at this time they felt to be childish and stupid, but they all doubtless possessed this sense of the situation in their mind. A young man thinks doggedly at such times. On the other hand, the ethics of their condition was decidedly against any open suggestion of hopelessness. So they were silent.

"Oh, well," said the captain, soothing his children, "we'll get ashore all right."

But there was that in his tone which made them think, so the oiler quoth: "Yes! If this wind holds!"

The cook was bailing: "Yes! If we don't catch hell in the surf."

Canton flannel gulls flew near and far. Sometimes they sat down on the sea, near patches of brown sea-weed that rolled over the waves with a movement like carpets on line in a gale. The birds sat comfortably in groups, and they were envied by some in the dingey, for the wrath of the sea was no more to them than it was to a covey of prairie chickens a thousand miles inland. Often they came very close and stared at the men with black bead-like eyes. At these times they were uncanny and sinister in their unblinking scrutiny, and the men hooted angrily at them, telling them to be gone. One came, and evidently decided to alight on the top of the captain's head. The bird flew parallel to the boat and did not circle, but made short sidelong jumps in the air in chicken-fashion. His black eyes were wistfully fixed upon the captain's head. "Ugly brute," said the oiler to the bird. "You look as if you were made with a jack-knife." The cook and the correspondent swore darkly at the creature. The captain naturally wished to knock it away with the end of the heavy painter, but he did not dare do it, because anything resembling an emphatic gesture would have capsized this freighted boat, and so with his open hand, the captain gently and carefully waved the gull away. After it had been discouraged from the pursuit the captain breathed easier on account of his hair, and others breathed easier because the bird struck their minds at this time as being somehow grewsome and ominous.

In the meantime the oiler and the correspondent rowed. And also they rowed.

They sat together in the same seat, and each rowed an oar. Then the oiler took both oars; then the correspondent took both oars; then the oiler; then the correspondent. They rowed and they rowed. The very ticklish part of the business was when the time came for the reclining one in the stern to take his turn at the oars. By the very last star of truth, it is easier to steal eggs from under a hen than it was to change seats in the dingey. First the man in the stern slid his hand along the thwart and moved with care, as if he were of Sevres. Then the man in the rowing seat slid his hand along the other thwart. It was all done with the most extraordinary care. As the two sidled past each other, the whole party kept watchful eyes on the coming wave, and the captain cried: "Look out now! Steady there!"

The brown mats of sea-weed that appeared from time to time were like islands, bits of earth. They were travelling, apparently, neither one way nor the other. They were, to all intents stationary. They informed the men in the boat that it was making progress slowly toward the land.

The captain, rearing cautiously in the bow, after the dingey soared on a great swell, said that he had seen the lighthouse at Mosquito Inlet. Presently the cook remarked that he had seen it. The correspondent was at the oars, then, and for some reason he too wished to look at the lighthouse, but his back was toward the far shore and the waves were important, and for some time he could not seize an opportunity to turn his head. But at last there came a wave more gentle than the others, and when at the crest of it he swiftly scoured the western horizon.

"See it?" said the captain.

"No," said the correspondent, slowly, "I didn't see anything."

"Look again," said the captain. He pointed. "It's exactly in that direction."

At the top of another wave, the correspondent did as he was bid, and this time his eyes chanced on a small still thing on the edge of the swaying horizon. It was precisely like the point of a pin. It took an anxious eye to find a lighthouse so tiny.

"Think we'll make it, captain?"

"If this wind holds and the boat don't swamp, we can't do much else," said the captain.

The little boat, lifted by each towering sea, and splashed viciously by the crests, made progress that in the absence of sea-weed was not apparent to those in her. She seemed just a wee thing wallowing, miraculously, top-up, at the mercy of five oceans. Occasionally, a great spread of water, like white flames, swarmed into her.

"Bail her, cook," said the captain, serenely.

"All right, captain," said the cheerful cook.

III

It would be difficult to describe the subtle brotherhood of men that was here established on the seas. No one said that it was so. No one mentioned it. But it dwelt in the boat, and each man felt it warm him. They were a captain, an oiler, a cook, and a correspondent, and they were friends, friends in a more curiously iron-bound degree than may be common. The hurt captain, lying against the water-jar in the bow, spoke always in a low voice and calmly, but he could never command a more ready and swiftly obedient crew than the motley three of the dingey. It was more than a mere recognition of what was best for the common safety. There was surely in it a quality that was personal and heartfelt. And after this devotion to the commander of the boat there was this comradeship that the correspondent, for instance, who had been taught to be cynical of men, knew even at the time was the best experience of his life. But no one said that it was so. No one mentioned it.

"I wish we had a sail," remarked the captain. "We might try my overcoat on the end of an oar and give you two boys a chance to rest." So the cook and the correspondent held the mast and spread wide the overcoat. The oiler steered, and the little boat made good way with her new rig. Sometimes the oiler had to scull sharply to keep a sea from breaking into the boat, but otherwise sailing was a success.

Meanwhile the light-house had been growing slowly larger. It had now almost assumed color, and appeared like a little gray shadow on the sky. The man at the oars could not be prevented from turning his head rather often to try for a glimpse of this little gray shadow.

At last, from the top of each wave the men in the tossing boat could see land. Even as the light-house was an upright shadow on the sky, this land seemed but a long black shadow on the sea. It certainly was thinner than paper. "We must be about opposite New Smyrna," said the cook, who had coasted this shore often in schooners. "Captain, by the way, I believe they abandoned that life-saving station there about a year ago."

"Did they?" said the captain.

The wind slowly died away. The cook and the correspondent were not now obliged to slave in order to hold high the oar. But the waves continued their old impetuous swooping at the dingey, and the little craft, no longer under way, struggled woundily over them. The oiler or the correspondent took the oars again.

Shipwrecks are apropos of nothing. If men could only train for them and have them occur when the men had reached pink condition, there would be less drowning at sea. Of the four in the dingey none had slept any time worth mentioning for two days and two nights previous to embarking in the dingey, and in the excitement of clambering about the deck of a foundering ship they had also forgotten to eat heartily.

For these reasons, and for others, neither the oiler nor the correspondent was fond of rowing at this time. The correspondent wondered ingenuously how in the name of all that was sane could there be people who thought it amusing to row a boat. It was not an amusement; it was a diabolical punishment, and even a genius of mental aberrations could never conclude that it was anything but a horror to the muscles and a crime against the back. He mentioned to the boat in general how the amusement of rowing struck him, and the weary-faced oiler smiled in full sympathy. Previously to the foundering, by the way, the oiler had worked double-watch in the engine-room of the ship.

"Take her easy, now, boys," said the captain. "Don't spend yourselves. If we have to run a surf you'll need all your strength, because we'll sure have to swim for it. Take your time."

Slowly the land arose from the sea. From a black line it became a line of black and a line of white, trees, and sand. Finally, the captain said that he could make out a house on the shore. "That's the house of refuge, sure," said the cook. "They'll see us before long, and come out after us."

The distant light-house reared high. "The keeper ought to be able to make us out now, if he's looking through a glass," said the captain. "He'll notify the life-saving people."

"None of those other boats could have got ashore to give word of the wreck," said the oiler, in a low voice. "Else the life-boat would be out hunting us."

Slowly and beautifully the land loomed out of the sea. The wind came again. It had veered from the northeast to the southeast. Finally, a new sound struck the ears of the men in the boat. It was the low thunder of the surf on the shore. "We'll never be able to make the light-house now," said the captain. "Swing her head a little more north, Billie," said the captain.

"'A little more north,' sir," said the oiler.

Whereupon the little boat turned her nose once more down the wind, and all but the oarsman watched the shore grow. Under the influence of this expansion doubt and direful apprehension was leaving the minds of the men. The management of the boat was still most absorbing, but it could not prevent a quiet cheerfulness. In an hour, perhaps, they would be ashore.

Their back-bones had become thoroughly used to balancing in the boat and they now rode this wild colt of a dingey like circus men. The correspondent thought that he had been drenched to the skin, but happening to feel in the top pocket of his coat, he found therein eight cigars. Four of them were soaked with sea-water; four were perfectly scatheless. After a search, somebody produced three dry matches, and thereupon the four waifs rode in their little boat, and with an assurance of an impending rescue shining in their eyes, puffed at the big cigars and judged well and ill of all men. Everybody took a drink of water.

IV

"Cook," remarked the captain, "there don't seem to be any signs of life about your house of refuge."

"No," replied the cook. "Funny they don't see us!"

A broad stretch of lowly coast lay before the eyes of the men. It was of low dunes topped with dark vegetation. The roar of the surf was plain, and sometimes they could see the white lip of a wave as it spun up the beach. A tiny house was blocked out black upon the sky. Southward, the slim light-house lifted its little gray length.

Tide, wind, and waves were swinging the dingey northward. "Funny they don't see us," said the men.

The surf's roar was here dulled, but its tone was, nevertheless, thunderous and mighty. As the boat swam over the great rollers, the men sat listening to this roar. "We'll swamp sure," said everybody.

It is fair to say here that there was not a life-saving station within twenty miles in either direction, but the men did not know this fact and in consequence they made dark and opprobrious remarks concerning the eyesight of the nation's life-savers. Four scowling men sat in the dingey and surpassed records in the invention of epithets.

"Funny they don't see us."

The light-heartedness of a former time had completely faded. To their sharpened minds it was easy to conjure pictures of all kinds of incompetency and blindness and indeed, cowardice. There was the shore of the populous land, and it was bitter and bitter to them that from it came no sign.

"Well," said the captain, ultimately, "I suppose we'll have to make a try for ourselves. If we stay out here too long, we'll none of us have strength left to swim after the boat swamps."

And so the oiler, who was at the oars, turned the boat straight for the shore. There was a sudden tightening of muscles. There was some thinking.

"If we don't all get ashore —" said the captain. "If we don't all get ashore, I suppose you fellows know where to send news of my finish?"

They then briefly exchanged some addresses and admonitions. As for the reflections of the men, there was a great deal of rage in them. Perchance they might be formulated thus: "If I am going to be drowned — if I am going to be drowned — if I am going to be drowned, why, in the name of the seven mad gods who rule the sea, was I allowed to come thus far and contemplate sand and trees? Was I brought here merely to have my nose dragged away as I was about to nibble the sacred cheese of life? It is preposterous. If this old ninny-woman, Fate, cannot do better than this, she should be deprived of the management of men's fortunes. She is an old hen who knows not her intention. If she has decided to drown me, why did she not do it in the beginning and save me all this trouble. The whole affair is absurd. . . . But, no, she cannot mean to drown me. She dare not drown me. She cannot drown me. Not after all this work." Afterward the man might have had an impulse to shake his fist at the clouds: "Just you drown me, now, and then hear what I call you!"

The billows that came at this time were more formidable. They seemed always just about to break and roll over the little boat in a turmoil of foam. There was a preparatory and long growl in the speech of them. No mind unused to the sea would have concluded that the dingey could ascend these sheer heights in time. The shore was still afar. The oiler was a wily surfman. "Boys," he said, swiftly, "she won't live three minutes more and we're too far out to swim. Shall I take her to sea again, captain?"

"Yes! Go ahead!" said the captain.

This oiler, by a series of quick miracles, and fast and steady oarsmanship, turned the boat in the middle of the surf and took her safely to sea again.

There was a considerable silence as the boat bumped over the furrowed sea to deeper water. Then somebody in gloom spoke. "Well, anyhow, they must have seen us from the shore by now."

The gulls went in slanting flight up the wind toward the gray desolate east. A squall, marked by dingy clouds, and clouds brick-red, like smoke from a burning building, appeared from the southeast.

"What do you think of those life-saving people? Ain't they peaches?"

"Funny they haven't seen us."

"Maybe they think we're out here for sport! Maybe they think we're fishin'. Maybe they think we're damned fools."

It was a long afternoon. A changed tide tried to force them southward, but wind and wave said northward. Far ahead, where coast-line, sea, and sky formed their mighty angle, there were little dots which seemed to indicate a city on the shore.

"St. Augustine?"

The captain shook his head. "Too near Mosquito Inlet."

And the oiler rowed, and then the correspondent rowed. Then the oiler rowed. It was a weary business. The human back can become the seat of more aches and pains than are registered in books for the composite anatomy of a regiment. It is a limited area, but it can become the theatre of innumerable muscular conflicts, tangles, wrenches, knots, and other comforts.

"Did you ever like to row, Billie?" asked the correspondent.

"No," said the oiler. "Hang it."

When one exchanged the rowing-seat for a place in the bottom of the boat, he suffered a bodily depression that caused him to be careless of everything save an obligation to wiggle one finger. There was cold sea-water swashing to and fro in the boat, and he lay in it. His head, pillowed on a thwart, was within an inch of the swirl of a wave crest, and sometimes a particularly obstreperous sea came in-board and drenched him once more. But these matters did not annoy him. It is almost certain that if the boat had capsized he would have tumbled comfortably out upon the ocean as if he felt sure it was a great soft mattress.

"Look! There's a man on the shore!"

"Where?"

"There! See 'im? See 'im?"

"Yes, sure! He's walking along."

"Now he's stopped. Look! He's facing us!"

"He's waving at us!"

"So he is! By thunder!"

"Ah, now, we're all right! Now we're all right! There'll be a boat out here for us in half an hour."

"He's going on. He's running. He's going up to that house there."

The remote beach seemed lower than the sea, and it required a searching glance to discern the little black figure. The captain saw a floating stick and they rowed to it. A bath-towel was by some weird chance in the boat, and, tying this on the stick, the captain waved it.

The oarsman did not dare turn his head, so he was obliged to ask questions.

"What's he doing now?"

"He's standing still again. He's looking, I think. . . . There he goes again. Toward the house. . . . Now he's stopped again."

"Is he waving at us?"

"No, not now! he was, though."

"Look! There comes another man!"

"He's running."

"Look at him go, would you."

"Why, he's on a bicycle. Now he's met the other man. They're both waving at us. Look!"

"There comes something up the beach."

"What the devil is that thing?"

"Why, it looks like a boat."

"Why, certainly it's a boat."

"No, it's on wheels."

"Yes, so it is. Well, that must be the life-boat. They drag them along shore on a wagon."

"That's the life-boat, sure."

"No, by — —, it's — it's an omnibus."

"I tell you it's a life-boat."

"It is not! It's an omnibus. I can see it plain. See? One of these big hotel omnibuses."

"By thunder, you're right. It's an omnibus, sure as fate. What do you suppose they are doing with an omnibus? Maybe they are going around collecting the life-crew, hey?"

"That's it, likely. Look! There's a fellow waving a little black flag. He's standing on the steps of the omnibus.

"There come those other two fellows. Now they're all talking together. Look at the fellow with the flag. Maybe he ain't waving it."

"That ain't a flag, is it? That's his coat. Why, certainly, that's his coat."

"So it is. It's his coat. He's taken it off and is waving it around his head. But would you look at him swing it."

"Oh, say, there isn't any life-saving station there. That's just a winter resort hotel omnibus that has brought over some of the boarders to see us drown."

"What's that idiot with the coat mean? What's he signaling, anyhow?"

"It looks as if he were trying to tell us to go north. There must be a life-saving station up there."

"No! He thinks we're fishing. Just giving us a merry hand. See? Ah, there, Willie."

"Well, I wish I could make something out of those signals. What do you suppose he means?"

"He don't mean anything. He's just playing."

"Well, if he'd just signal us to try the surf again, or to go to sea and wait, or go north, or go south, or go to hell — there would be some reason in it. But look at him. He just stands there and keeps his coat revolving like a wheel. The ass!"

"There come more people."

"Now there's quite a mob. Look! Isn't that a boat?"

"Where? Oh, I see where you mean. No, that's no boat."

"That fellow is still waving his coat."

"He must think we like to see him do that. Why don't he quit it. It don't mean anything."

"I don't know. I think he is trying to make us go north. It must be that there's a life-saving station there somewhere."

"Say, he ain't tired yet. Look at 'im wave."

"Wonder how long he can keep that up. He's been revolving his coat ever since he caught sight of us. He's an idiot. Why aren't they getting men to bring a boat out. A fishing boat — one of those big yawls — could come out here all right. Why don't he do something?"

"Oh, it's all right, now."

"They'll have a boat out here for us in less than no time, now that they've seen us."

A faint yellow tone came into the sky over the low land. The shadows on the sea slowly deepened. The wind bore coldness with it, and the men began to shiver.

"Holy smoke!" said one, allowing his voice to express his impious mood, "if we keep on monkeying out here! If we've got to flounder out here all night!"

"Oh, we'll never have to stay here all night! Don't you worry. They've seen us now, and it won't be long before they'll come chasing out after us."

The shore grew dusky. The man waving a coat blended gradually into this gloom, and it swallowed in the same manner the omnibus and the group of people. The spray, when it dashed uproariously over the side, made the voyagers shrink and swear like men who were being branded.

"I'd like to catch the chump who waved the coat. I feel like soaking him one, just for luck."

"Why? What did he do?"

"Oh, nothing, but then he seemed so damned cheerful."

In the meantime the oiler rowed, and then the correspondent rowed, and then the oiler rowed. Gray-faced and bowed forward, they mechanically, turn by turn, plied the leaden oars. The form of the light-house had vanished from the southern horizon, but finally a pale star appeared, just lifting from the sea. The streaked saffron in the west passed before the all-merging darkness, and the sea to the east was black. The land had vanished, and was expressed only by the low and drear thunder of the surf.

"If I am going to be drowned—if I am going to be drowned—if I am going to be drowned, why, in the name of the seven mad gods, who rule the sea, was I allowed to come thus far and contemplate sand and trees? Was I brought here merely to have my nose dragged away as I was about to nibble the sacred cheese of life?"

The patient captain, drooped over the water-jar, was sometimes obliged to speak to the oarsman.

"Keep her head up! Keep her head up!"

"'Keep her head up,' sir." The voices were weary and low.

This was surely a quiet evening. All save the oarsman lay heavily and listlessly in the boat's bottom. As for him, his eyes were just capable of noting the tall black waves that swept forward in a most sinister silence, save for an occasional subdued growl of a crest.

The cook's head was on a thwart, and he looked without interest at the water under his nose. He was deep in other scenes. Finally he spoke. "Billie," he murmured, dreamfully, "what kind of pie do you like best?"

V

"Pie," said the oiler and the correspondent, agitatedly. "Don't talk about those things, blast you!"

"Well," said the cook, "I was just thinking about ham sandwiches, and—"

A night on the sea in an open boat is a long night. As darkness settled finally, the shine of the light, lifting from the sea in the south, changed to full gold. On the northern horizon a new light appeared, a small bluish gleam on the edge of the waters. These two lights were the furniture of the world. Otherwise there was nothing but waves.

Two men huddled in the stern, and distances were so magnificent in the dingey that the rower was enabled to keep his feet partly warmed by thrusting them under his companions. Their legs indeed extended far under the rowing-seat until they touched the feet of the captain forward. Sometimes, despite the efforts of the tired oarsman, a wave came piling into the boat, an icy wave of the night, and the chilling water soaked them anew. They would twist their bodies for a moment and groan, and sleep the dead sleep once more, while the water in the boat gurgled about them as the craft rocked.

The plan of the oiler and the correspondent was for one to row until he lost the ability, and then arouse the other from his sea-water couch in the bottom of the boat.

The oiler plied the oars until his head drooped forward, and the overpowering sleep blinded him. And he rowed yet afterward. Then he touched a man in the bottom of the boat, and called his name. "Will you spell me for a little while?" he said, meekly.

"Sure, Billie," said the correspondent, awakening and dragging himself to a sitting position. They exchanged places carefully, and the oiler, cuddling down to the sea-water at the cook's side, seemed to go to sleep instantly.

The particular violence of the sea had ceased. The waves came without snarling. The obligation of the man at the oars was to keep the boat headed so that the tilt of the rollers would not capsize her, and to preserve her from filling when the crests rushed past. The black waves were silent and hard to be seen in the darkness. Often one was almost upon the boat before the oarsman was aware.

In a low voice the correspondent addressed the captain. He was not sure that the captain was awake, although this iron man seemed to be always awake. "Captain, shall I keep her making for that light north, sir?"

The same steady voice answered him. "Yes. Keep it about two points off the port bow."

The cook had tied a life-belt around himself in order to get even the warmth which this clumsy cork contrivance could donate, and he seemed almost stove-like when a rower, whose teeth invariably chattered wildly as soon as he ceased his labor, dropped down to sleep.

The correspondent, as he rowed, looked down at the two men sleeping under foot. The cook's arm was around the oiler's shoulders, and, with their fragmentary clothing and haggard faces, they were the babes of the sea, a grotesque rendering of the old babes in the wood.

Later he must have grown stupid at his work, for suddenly there was a growling of water, and a crest came with a roar and a swash into the boat, and it was a wonder that it did not set the cook afloat in his life-belt. The cook continued to sleep, but the oiler sat up, blinking his eyes and shaking with the new cold.

"Oh, I'm awful sorry, Billie," said the correspondent, contritely.

"That's all right, old boy," said the oiler, and lay down again and was asleep.

Presently it seemed that even the captain dozed, and the correspondent thought that he was the one man afloat on all the oceans. The wind had a voice as it came over the waves, and it was sadder than the end.

There was a long, loud swishing astern of the boat, and a gleaming trail of phosphorescence, like blue flame, was furrowed on the black waters. It might have been made by a monstrous knife.

Then there came a stillness, while the correspondent breathed with the open mouth and looked at the sea.

Suddenly there was another swish and another long flash of bluish light, and this time it was alongside the boat, and might almost have been reached with an oar. The correspondent saw an enormous fin speed like a shadow through the water, hurling the crystalline spray and leaving the long glowing trail.

The correspondent looked over his shoulder at the captain. His face was hidden, and he seemed to be asleep. He looked at the babes of the sea. They certainly were asleep. So, being bereft of sympathy, he leaned a little way to one side and swore softly into the sea.

But the thing did not then leave the vicinity of the boat. Ahead or astern, on one side or the other, at intervals long or short, fled the long sparkling streak, and there was to be heard the whirroo of the dark fin. The speed and power of the thing was greatly to be admired. It cut the water like a gigantic and keen projectile.

The presence of this biding thing did not affect the man with the same horror that it would if he had been a picnicker. He simply looked at the sea dully and swore in an undertone.

Nevertheless, it is true that he did not wish to be alone with the thing. He wished one of his companions to awaken by chance and keep him company with it. But the captain hung motionless over the water-jar and the oiler and the cook in the bottom of the boat were plunged in slumber.

VI

"If I am going to be drowned — if I am going to be drowned — if I am going to be drowned, why, in the name of the seven mad gods, who rule the sea, was I allowed to come thus far and contemplate sand and trees?"

During this dismal night, it may be remarked that a man would conclude that it was really the intention of the seven mad gods to drown him, despite the abominable injustice of it. For it was certainly an abominable injustice to drown a man who had worked so hard, so hard. The man felt it would be a crime most unnatural. Other people had drowned at sea since galleys swarmed with painted sails, but still —

When it occurs to a man that nature does not regard him as important, and that she feels she would not maim the universe by disposing of him, he at first wishes to throw bricks at the temple, and he hates deeply the fact that there are no bricks and no temples. Any visible expression of nature would surely be pelleted with his jeers.

Then, if there be no tangible thing to hoot he feels, perhaps, the desire to confront a personification and indulge in pleas, bowed to one knee, and with hands supplicant, saying: "Yes, but I love myself."

A high cold star on a winter's night is the word he feels that she says to him. Thereafter he knows the pathos of his situation.

The men in the dingey had not discussed these matters, but each had, no doubt, reflected upon them in silence and according to his mind. There was seldom any expression upon their faces save the general one of complete weariness. Speech was devoted to the business of the boat.

To chime the notes of his emotion, a verse mysteriously entered the correspondent's head. He had even forgotten that he had forgotten this verse, but it suddenly was in his mind.

A soldier of the Legion lay dying in Algiers; There was lack of woman's nursing, there was dearth of woman's tears; But a comrade stood beside him, and he took that comrade's hand. And he said: "I shall never see my own, my native land."

In his childhood, the correspondent had been made acquainted with the fact that a soldier of the Legion lay dying in Algiers, but he had never regarded the fact as important. Myriads of his school-fellows had informed him of the soldier's plight, but the dinning had naturally ended by making him perfectly indifferent. He had never considered it his affair that a soldier of the Legion lay dying in Algiers, nor had it appeared to him as a matter for sorrow. It was less to him than breaking of a pencil's point.

Now, however, it quaintly came to him as a human, living thing. It was no longer merely a picture of a few throes in the breast of a poet, meanwhile drinking tea and warming his feet at the grate; it was an actuality — stern, mournful, and fine.

The correspondent plainly saw the soldier. He lay on the sand with his feet out straight and still. While his pale left hand was upon his chest in an attempt to thwart the going of his life, the blood came between his fingers. In the far Algerian distance, a city of low square forms was set against a sky that was faint with the last sunset hues. The correspondent, plying the oars and dreaming of the slow and slower movements of the lips of the soldier, was moved by a profound and perfectly impersonal comprehension. He was sorry for the soldier of the Legion who lay dying in Algiers.

The thing which had followed the boat and waited had evidently grown bored at the delay. There was no longer to be heard the slash of the cut-water, and there was no longer the flame of the long trail. The light in the north still glimmered, but it was apparently no nearer to the boat. Sometimes the boom of the surf rang in the correspondent's ears, and he turned the craft seaward then and rowed harder. Southward, someone had evidently built a watch-fire on the beach. It was too low and too far to be seen, but it made a shimmering, roseate reflection upon the bluff back of it, and this could be discerned from the boat. The wind came stronger, and sometimes a wave suddenly raged out like a mountain-cat and there was to be seen the sheen and sparkle of a broken crest.

The captain, in the bow, moved on his water-jar and sat erect. "Pretty long night," he observed to the correspondent. He looked at the shore. "Those life-saving people take their time."

"Did you see that shark playing around?"

"Yes, I saw him. He was a big fellow, all right."

"Wish I had known you were awake."

Later the correspondent spoke into the bottom of the boat.

"Billie!" There was a slow and gradual disentanglement. "Billie, will you spell me?"

"Sure," said the oiler.

As soon as the correspondent touched the cold comfortable sea-water in the bottom of the boat, and had huddled close to the cook's life-belt he was deep in sleep, despite the fact that his teeth played all the popular airs. This sleep was so good to him that it was but a moment before he heard a voice call his name in a tone that demonstrated the last stages of exhaustion. "Will you spell me?"

"Sure, Billie."

The light in the north had mysteriously vanished, but the correspondent took his course from the wide-awake captain.

Later in the night they took the boat farther out to sea, and the captain directed the cook to take one oar at the stern and keep the boat facing the seas. He was to call out if he should hear the thunder of the surf. This plan enabled the oiler and the correspondent to get respite together. "We'll give those boys a chance to get into shape again," said the captain. They curled down and, after a few preliminary chatterings and trembles, slept once more the dead sleep. Neither knew they had bequeathed to the cook the company of another shark, or perhaps the same shark.

As the boat caroused on the waves, spray occasionally bumped over the side and gave them a fresh soaking, but this had no power to break their repose. The ominous slash of the wind and the water affected them as it would have affected mummies.

"Boys," said the cook, with the notes of every reluctance in his voice, "she's drifted in pretty close. I guess one of you had better take her to sea again." The correspondent, aroused, heard the crash of the toppled crests.

As he was rowing, the captain gave him some whiskey and water, and this steadied the chills out of him. "If I ever get ashore and anybody shows me even a photograph of an oar—"

At last there was a short conversation.

"Billie. . . . Billie, will you spell me?"

"Sure," said the oiler.

VII

When the correspondent again opened his eyes, the sea and the sky were each of the gray hue of the dawning. Later, carmine and gold was painted upon the waters. The morning appeared finally, in its splendor with a sky of pure blue, and the sunlight flamed on the tips of the waves.

On the distant dunes were set many little black cottages, and a tall white wind-mill reared above them. No man, nor dog, nor bicycle appeared on the beach. The cottages might have formed a deserted village.

The voyagers scanned the shore. A conference was held in the boat. "Well," said the captain, "if no help is coming, we might better try a run through the surf right away. If we stay out here much longer we will be too weak to do anything for ourselves at all." The others silently acquiesced in this reasoning. The boat was headed for the beach. The correspondent wondered if none ever ascended the tall wind-tower, and if then they never looked seaward. This tower was a giant, standing with its back to the plight of the ants. It represented in a degree, to the correspondent, the serenity of nature amid the struggles of the individual—nature in the wind, and nature in the vision of men. She did not seem cruel to him, nor beneficent, nor treacherous, nor wise. But she was indifferent, flatly indifferent. It is, perhaps, plausible that a man in this situation, impressed with the unconcern of the universe, should see the innumerable flaws of his life and have them taste wickedly in his mind and wish for another chance. A distinction between right and wrong seems absurdly clear to him, then, in this new ignorance of the grave-edge, and he understands that if he were given another opportunity he would mend his conduct and his words, and be better and brighter during an introduction, or at a tea.

"Now, boys," said the captain, "she is going to swamp sure. All we can do is to work her in as far as possible, and then when she swamps, pile out and scramble for the beach. Keep cool now and don't jump until she swamps sure."

The oiler took the oars. Over his shoulders he scanned the surf. "Captain," he said, "I think I'd better bring her about, and keep her head-on to the seas and back her in."

"All right, Billie," said the captain. "Back her in." The oiler swung the boat then and, seated in the stern, the cook and the correspondent were obliged to look over their shoulders to contemplate the lonely and indifferent shore.

The monstrous inshore rollers heaved the boat high until the men were again enabled to see the white sheets of water scudding up the slanted beach. "We won't get in very close," said the captain. Each time a man could wrest his attention from the rollers, he turned his glance toward the shore, and in the expression of the eyes during this contemplation there was a singular quality. The correspondent, observing the others, knew that they were not afraid, but the full meaning of their glances was shrouded.

As for himself, he was too tired to grapple fundamentally with the fact. He tried to coerce his mind into thinking of it, but the mind was dominated at this time by the muscles, and the muscles said they did not care. It merely occurred to him that if he should drown it would be a shame.

There were no hurried words, no pallor, no plain agitation. The men simply looked at the shore. "Now, remember to get well clear of the boat when you jump," said the captain.

Seaward the crest of a roller suddenly fell with a thunderous crash, and the long white comber came roaring down upon the boat.

"Steady now," said the captain. The men were silent. They turned their eyes from the shore to the comber and waited. The boat slid up the incline, leaped at the furious top, bounced over it, and swung down the long back of the waves. Some water had been shipped and the cook bailed it out.

But the next crest crashed also. The tumbling boiling flood of white water caught the boat and whirled it almost perpendicular. Water swarmed in from all sides. The correspondent had his hands on the gunwale at this time, and when the water entered at that place he swiftly withdrew his fingers, as if he objected to wetting them.

The little boat, drunken with this weight of water, reeled and snuggled deeper into the sea.

"Bail her out, cook! Bail her out," said the captain.

"All right, captain," said the cook.

"Now, boys, the next one will do for us, sure," said the oiler. "Mind to jump clear of the boat."

The third wave moved forward, huge, furious, implacable. It fairly swallowed the dingey, and almost simultaneously the men tumbled into the sea. A piece of life-belt had lain in the bottom of the boat, and as the correspondent went overboard he held this to his chest with his left hand.

The January water was icy, and he reflected immediately that it was colder than he had expected to find it off the coast of Florida. This appeared to his dazed mind as a fact important enough to be noted at the time. The coldness of the water was sad; it was tragic. This fact was somehow mixed and confused with his opinion of his own situation that it seemed almost a proper reason for tears. The water was cold.

When he came to the surface he was conscious of little but the noisy water. Afterward he saw his companions in the sea. The oiler was ahead in the race. He was swimming strongly and rapidly. Off to the correspondent's left, the cook's great white and corked back bulged out of the water, and in the rear the captain was hanging with his one good hand to the keel of the overturned dingey.

There is a certain immovable quality to a shore, and the correspondent wondered at it amid the confusion of the sea.

It seemed also very attractive, but the correspondent knew that it was a long journey, and he paddled leisurely. The piece of life-preserver lay under him, and sometimes he whirled down the incline of a wave as if he were on a hand-sled.

But finally he arrived at a place in the sea where travel was beset with difficulty. He did not pause swimming to inquire what manner of current had caught him, but there his progress ceased. The shore was set before him like a bit of scenery on a stage, and he looked at it and understood with his eyes each detail of it.

As the cook passed, much farther to the left, the captain was calling to him, "Turn over on your back, cook! Turn over on your back and use the oar."

"All right, sir!" The cook turned on his back, and, paddling with an oar, went ahead as if he were a canoe.

Presently the boat also passed to the left of the correspondent with the captain clinging with one hand to the keel. He would have appeared like a man raising himself to look over a board fence, if it were not for the extraordinary gymnastics of the boat. The correspondent marvelled that the captain could still hold to it.

They passed on, nearer to shore—the oiler, the cook, the captain—and following them went the water-jar, bouncing gayly over the seas.

The correspondent remained in the grip of this strange new enemy—a current. The shore, with its white slope of sand and its green bluff, topped with little silent cottages, was spread like a picture before him. It was very near to him then, but he was impressed as one who in a gallery looks at a scene from Brittany or Algiers.

He thought: "I am going to drown? Can it be possible? Can it be possible? Can it be possible?" Perhaps an individual must consider his own death to be the final phenomenon of nature.

But later a wave perhaps whirled him out of this small deadly current, for he found suddenly that he could again make progress toward the shore. Later still, he was aware that the captain, clinging with one hand to the keel of the dingey, had his face turned away from the shore and toward him, and was calling his name. "Come to the boat! Come to the boat!"

In his struggle to reach the captain and the boat, he reflected that when one gets properly wearied, drowning must really be a comfortable arrangement, a cessation of hostilities accompanied by a large degree of relief, and he was glad of it, for the main thing in his mind for some moments had been horror of the temporary agony. He did not wish to be hurt.

Presently he saw a man running along the shore. He was undressing with most remarkable speed. Coat, trousers, shirt, everything flew magically off him.

"Come to the boat," called the captain.

"All right, captain." As the correspondent paddled, he saw the captain let himself down to bottom and leave the boat. Then the correspondent performed his one little marvel of the voyage. A large wave caught him and flung him with ease and supreme speed completely over the boat and far beyond it. It struck him even then as an event in gymnastics, and a true miracle of the sea. An overturned boat in the surf is not a plaything to a swimming man.

The correspondent arrived in water that reached only to his waist, but his condition did not enable him to stand for more than a moment. Each wave knocked him into a heap, and the under-tow pulled at him.

Then he saw the man who had been running and undressing, and undressing and running, come bounding into the water. He dragged ashore the cook, and then waded toward the captain, but the captain waved him away, and sent him to the correspondent. He was naked, naked as a tree in winter, but a halo was about his head, and he shone like a saint. He gave a strong pull, and a long drag, and a bully heave at the correspondent's hand. The correspondent, schooled in the minor formulae, said: "Thanks, old man." But suddenly the man cried: "What's that?" He pointed a swift finger. The correspondent said: "Go."

In the shallows, face downward, lay the oiler. His forehead touched sand that was periodically, between each wave, clear of the sea.

The correspondent did not know all that transpired afterward. When he achieved safe ground he fell, striking the sand with each particular part of his body. It was as if he had dropped from a roof, but the thud was grateful to him.

It seems that instantly the beach was populated with men with blankets, clothes, and flasks, and women with coffee-pots and all the remedies sacred to their minds. The welcome of the land to the men from the sea was warm and generous, but a still and dripping shape was carried slowly up the beach, and the land's welcome for it could only be the different and sinister hospitality of the grave.

When it came night, the white waves paced to and fro in the moonlight, and the wind brought the sound of the great sea's voice to the men on shore, and they felt that they could then be interpreters.

— End —

Questions for Critical Thinking and Writing

1. In section IV, the narration is broken somewhat by long strings of dialogue not attributed to any specific character. What is the significance of this scene? Why do the characters refuse to give up hope that they will be rescued?

2. What is the significance of the seagull that lands on the captain's head on page 34? What does this scene symbolize, in your opinion?

3. Why isn't the death of the oiler expanded? What does the lack of explanation imply about the worth of the oiler's life?

4. On page 48, as they are finally trying to make it to shore, the correspondent is lifted over the boat by a wave, which "struck him even then as an event in gymnastics, and a true miracle of the sea." How does this description of a wave compare to the waves throughout the rest of the story?

BETTY SUE CUMMINGS

Betty Sue Cummings was born in 1918 in Big Stone Gap, Virginia. After receiving her B.S. from Longwood College in 1939 and her M.A. from the University of Washington, Seattle, in 1949, she became an English teacher and counselor in Titusville, Florida. Before her death in 2001, Cummings was nominated for a National Book Award for Children's Literature.

BEFORE YOU READ

Say These Names (Remember Them) emphasizes the importance not only of knowing one's history but also of being able to repeat that history. How do oral traditions differ from written traditions, and what is the importance of language in a culture?

From *Say These Names (Remember Them)*   1984

When See-ho-kee was a small girl, she asked her grandmother a question. "Who am I?"

Her grandmother gave her a look of alertness and sharp focus, and See-ho-kee was surprised at the length of her answer.

"You are See-ho-kee. You are Yakitisee—red person. You are Miccosukee. You are of the important Wind clan. Women of the Wind clan are called the grandmothers of the tribe. I am *everybody's* grandmother. So is your mother, and so will you be. As a member of the Wind clan, you will be allowed to take up the club against adulterers even after the club has been used up to four times."

"I don't want to do that."

"In the old days we did it," her grandmother said sternly, "and there was not much adultery either."

She shook her head with vexation and went on with her answer. "According to the white people you are Seminole, because your people left the northern villages and came here to Florida.

"You are Hitch-e-tee. You speak Mikasuki. I used to speak Mus-ko-gee Creek as well, and now the Creeks fight against us with the white man. You are Creek from the Coo-sau and the Tal-la-poo-sa and also from the Chat-to-ho-che. We traveled those creeks and knew each other in the old times. Our warriors fought each other, some for white Americans, some against. We will be brothers and sisters again, all against the whites.

"You are your parents' daughter, part of them. You are my granddaughter. You are part of the Che-au-haus. My grandmother lived in their village."

The old woman hesitated, and her sharp look softened. Tears suddenly went down her cheeks.

"You are part of all the villages I used to know."

"What villages?" See-ho-kee asked. "Have I been there?"

"No. Those villages are dead now. No one lives there. Those people came here or went west. Or died. Still, you are part of them."

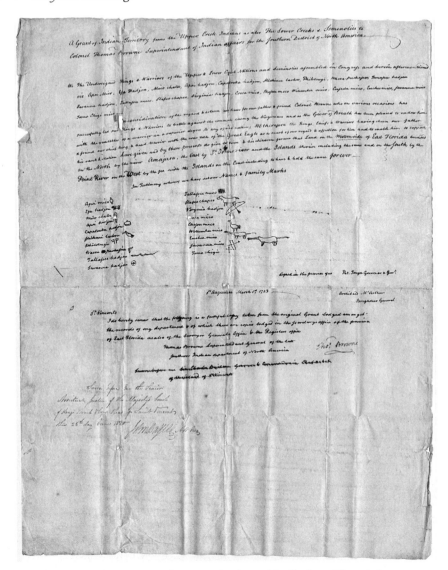

Land Grant from the Upper Creeks, Lower Creeks, and Seminoles to Thomas Brown, March 1, 1783 (1820 copy). The State Archives of Florida explains this document: "In 1774, Thomas Brown came to North America from England to establish a plantation in the Georgia backcountry. Brown quickly became embroiled in rising tensions between loyalists and rebels leading up to the outbreak of the Revolutionary War. . . . During his campaigns, Brown gained the support and assistance of several Creek and Seminole Indian leaders. They provided warriors to fight the mutual enemy, the Americans, and in return the Englishman Brown kept their towns well-armed and provisioned. . . . What is most significant about this document is not its association with Thomas Brown. This document contains rare illustrations of southeastern Indian clan symbols. . . . Because of the inclusion of clan symbols, this document seems to suggest that clan was at least as important as town for these particular Creek and Seminole leaders. It is also significant that Upper Creeks, Lower Creeks and the Seminoles united in their appreciation of Thomas Brown, although it is unclear why the grant implicated only lands in Florida belonging to the Seminoles and not Creek territory in Alabama and Georgia."
Courtesy of the State Archives of Florida.

"What are the villages?" See-ho-kee persisted. Her grandmother threw her head back and sang the names so fast that See-ho-kee's ears refused to hear. "You should remember those names," her grandmother told her. "How can I remember them when I can't even say them?" See-ho-kee asked. And this was the beginning of her grandmother's stomp-dance and name-song, for her grandmother was determined to have See-ho-kee learn the names of her ancestors' villages.

QUESTIONS FOR CRITICAL THINKING AND WRITING

1. How does See-ho-kee's grandmother's description of her granddaughter's ancestry differ from that assigned by white colonists?

2. Why might the grandmother want See-ho-kee to learn how to speak her tribe's name and learn the tribe's language?

3. See-ho-kee's relatively short question — "Who am I?" — elicited a surprisingly long answer from her grandmother. Why might the grandmother think this is such an important question, and how does she define who See-ho-kee is?

4. **CONNECT TO ANOTHER READING.** Both Betty Sue Cummings and J. Russell Reaver (p. 107) assign great importance to speech. Looking at this excerpt from *Say These Names (Remember Them)* and the assorted folktales collected by Reaver, in a short essay compare and contrast the dialect and method of storytelling used in each case.

SILVIA CURBELO

Silvia Curbelo (b. 1955) is a Cuban American poet and writer who has published three collections of poetry to date. She has received multiple fellowships for her poetry, and in 1996 she won the Jessica Nobel-Maxwell memorial prize from the *American Poetry Review*. She lives in Tampa, Florida, and is an editor for *Organica* magazine.

Courtesy of Silvia Curbelo.

BEFORE YOU READ

"For All the Goodbyes" is arranged in couplets. As you read, examine how the couplets affect the pauses you take in reading, and how the white space adds emphasis to certain phrases. How would the meaning or the emphasis in the poem change if it weren't arranged in couplets?

For All the Goodbyes 1991

In a room not unlike this one
someone is always leaving someone else.

Someone blows out a candle.
Someone has finished the wine.

The single glove laid open 5
on the windowsill tells only

half the story. Try to imagine
the hundred metaphors for flight,

for endings, a door finally closing
and what is left behind— 10

the robe with its torn lining,
a scarf, cufflinks, an old shoe.

A man's abandoned overcoat
brings to mind

train stations, suitcases, 15
footsteps vanishing down the hall.

There is no mistaking
the closet door left ajar,

the empty hangers
like the thin shoulders 20

of loss, of distance.
If you have loved

someone like that
you have imagined his hands

opening other doors, unbuttoning 25
his shirt in other rooms.

Even as the buttons fall away
there is no turning back.

A dropped shoe is an island.
A scarf will break your heart. 30

QUESTIONS FOR CRITICAL THINKING AND WRITING

1. In the fourth stanza, Curbelo speaks directly to the reader, commanding, "Try to imagine / the hundred metaphors for flight." Why might Curbelo have wanted to speak directly to the reader, and what effect does this decision have on the tone of the poem?

2. What type of loss is Curbelo talking about in her poem? What makes you think so? Cite specific lines.

3. In the last stanza, Curbelo writes, "A dropped shoe is an island." What might Curbelo mean by this line? Try to examine multiple meanings, if possible.

JOAN DIDION

Joan Didion (b. 1934) is an American writer
known for her essays, fiction, and screenplays.
She got her start in magazines, working as a
feature editor for *Vogue* and writing for various other publications like *Esquire* and *Life*. In
2005, she won the National Book Award for *The
Year of Magical Thinking*, which she later adapted
into a one-woman play on Broadway, starring
Vanessa Redgrave.

Courtesy of Julian Wasser/Getty
Images.

BEFORE YOU READ

Joan Didion exposes another side of Florida in the following essay—that
of violence and drug running in Miami. It is, of course, more common to
idealize the natural environment of Florida, but Didion uses the tropical,
swampy nature to symbolize the way crime can seep into a community. As
you read, think about the way Didion tries to portray Miami. How does it
compare to your idea of Miami, and do you think it is an accurate representation of the city?

From *Miami*   *1987*

During the spring when I began visiting Miami all of Florida was reported
to be in drought, with dropping water tables and unfilled aquifers and
SAVE WATER signs, but drought, in a part of the world which would be in its
natural state a shelf of porous oolitic limestone covered most of the year by
a shallow sheet flow of fresh water, proved relative. During this drought the
city of Coral Gables continued, as it had every night since 1924, to empty and
refill its Venetian Pool with fresh unchlorinated water, 820,000 gallons a day
out of the water supply and into the storm sewer. There was less water than
there might have been in the Biscayne Aquifer but there was water everywhere
above it. There were rains so hard that windshield wipers stopped working
and cars got swamped and stalled on I-95. There was water roiling and bub-
bling over the underwater lights in decorative pools. There was water sluicing
off the six-story canted window at the Omni, a hotel from which it was possible to see, in the Third World way, both the slums of Overtown and those
island houses with the Unusual Security and Ready Access to the Ocean,
equally wet. Water plashed off banana palms, water puddled on flat roofs,
water streamed down the CARNE U.S. GOOD & U.S. STANDARD signs on Flagler
Street. Water rocked the impounded drug boats which lined the Miami River
and water lapped against the causeways on the bay. I got used to the smell of
incipient mildew in my clothes. I stuffed Kleenex in wet shoes and stopped
expecting them to dry.

A certain liquidity suffused everything about the place. Causeways and
bridges and even Brickell Avenue did not stay put but rose and fell, allowing

the masts of ships to glide among the marble and glass facades of the unleased office buildings. The buildings themselves seemed to swim free against the sky: there had grown up in Miami during the recent money years an architecture which appeared to have slipped its moorings, a not inappropriate style for a terrain with only a provisional claim on being land at all. Surfaces were reflective, opalescent. Angles were oblique, intersecting to disorienting effect. The Arquitectonica office, which produced the celebrated glass condominium on Brickell Avenue with the fifty-foot cube cut from its center, the frequently photographed "sky patio" in which there floated a palm tree, a Jacuzzi, and a lipstick-red spiral staircase, accompanied its elevations with crayon sketches, all moons and starry skies and airborne maidens, as in a Chagall. Skidmore, Owings and Merrill managed, in its Southeast Financial Center, the considerable feat of rendering fifty-five stories of polished gray granite incorporeal, a sky-blue illusion.

Nothing about Miami was exactly fixed, or hard. Hard consonants were missing from the local speech patterns, in English as well as in Spanish. Local money tended to move on hydraulic verbs: when it was not being washed it was being diverted, or channeled through Mexico, or turned off in Washington. Local stories tended to turn on underwater plot points, submerged snappers: on unsoundable extradition proceedings in the Bahamas, say, or fluid connections with the Banco Nacional de Colombia. I recall trying to touch the bottom of one such story in the *Herald*, about six hand grenades which had just been dug up in the bay-front backyard of a Biscayne Boulevard pawnbroker who had been killed in his own bed a few years before, shot at close range with a .25-caliber automatic pistol.

There were some other details on the surface of this story; for example, the wife who fired the .25-caliber automatic pistol and the nineteen-year-old daughter who was up on federal weapons charges and the flight attendant who rented the garage apartment and said that the pawnbroker had collected "just basic things like rockets, just defused things," but the underwater narrative included, at last sounding, the Central Intelligence Agency (with which the pawnbroker was said to have been associated), the British intelligence agency MI6 (with which the pawnbroker was also said to have been associated), the late Anastasio Somoza Debayle (whose family the pawnbroker was said to have spirited into Miami shortly before the regime fell in Managua), the late shah of Iran (whose presence in Panama was said to have queered an arms deal about which the pawnbroker had been told), Dr. Josef Mengele (for whom the pawnbroker was said to be searching), and a Pompano Beach resident last seen cruising Miami in a cinnamon-colored Cadillac Sedan de Ville and looking to buy, he said for the Salvadoran insurgents, a million rounds of ammunition, thirteen thousand assault rifles, and "at least a couple" of jeep-mounted machine guns.

In this mood Miami seemed not a city at all but a tale, a romance of the tropics, a kind of waking dream in which any possibility could and would be accommodated. The most ordinary morning, say at the courthouse, could open onto the distinctly lurid. "I don't think he came out with me, that's all," I recall hearing someone say one day in an elevator at the Miami federal courthouse. His voice had kept rising. "What happened to all that stuff about how next time, he gets twenty keys, he could run wherever-it-is-Idaho, now he says he wouldn't know what to do with five keys, what is this shit?" His companion had shrugged. We had continued in silence to the main floor. Outside one courtroom that day a group of Colombians, the women in silk shirts and Chanel necklaces and Charles Jourdan suede pumps, the children in appliquéd dresses from Baby Dior, had been waiting for the decision in a pretrial detention hearing, one in which the government was contending that the two defendants, who between them lived in houses in which eighty-three kilos of cocaine and a million-three in cash had been found, failed to qualify as good bail risks.

"That doesn't make him a longtime drug dealer," one of the two defense lawyers, both of whom were Anglo and one of whom drove a Mercedes 380 SEL with the license plate DEFENSE, had argued about the million-three in cash. "That could be one transaction." Across the hall that day closing arguments were being heard in a boat case, a "boat case" being one in which a merchant or fishing vessel has been boarded and drugs seized and eight or ten Colombian crew members arrested, the kind of case in which pleas were typically entered so that one of the Colombians would get eighteen months and the others deported. There were never any women in Chanel necklaces around a boat case, and the lawyers (who were usually hired and paid for not by the defendants but by the unnamed owner of the "load," or shipment) tended to be Cuban. "You had the great argument, you got to give me some good ideas," one of the eight Cuban defense lawyers on this case joked with the prosecutor during a recess. "But you haven't heard my argument yet," another of the defense lawyers said. "The stuff about communism. Fabulous closing argument."

Just as any morning could turn lurid, any moment could turn final, again as in a dream. "I heard a loud, short noise and then there was just a plain moment of dullness," the witness to a shooting in a Miami Beach supermarket parking lot told the *Herald*. "There was no one around except me and two bagboys." I happened to be in the coroner's office one morning when autopsies were being performed on the bodies of two Mariels, shot and apparently pushed from a car on I-95 about nine the evening before, another plain moment of dullness. The story had been on television an hour or two after it happened: I had seen the crime site on the eleven o'clock news, and had not expected to see the victims in the morning. "When he came here in Mariel he stayed at our house but he didn't get along with my mom," a young girl was saying in the anteroom to one of the detectives working the case. "These two guys were killed together," the detective had pressed. "They probably knew each other."

"For sure," the young girl had said, agreeably. Inside the autopsy room the hands of the two young men were encased in the brown paper bags which indicated that the police had not yet taken what they needed for laboratory studies. Their flesh had the marbleized yellow look of the recently dead. There were other bodies in the room, in various stages of autopsy, and a young woman in a white coat taking eyes, for the eye bank. "Who are we going to start on next?" one of the assistant medical examiners was saying. "The fat guy? Let's do the fat guy."

It was even possible to enter the waking dream without leaving the house, just by reading the *Herald*. A Mariel named Jose "Coca-Cola" Yero gets arrested, with nine acquaintances, in a case involving 1,664 pounds of cocaine, a thirty-seven-foot Cigarette boat named *The Connection*, two Lamborghinis, a million-six in cash, a Mercedes 500 SEL with another $350,000 in cash in the trunk, one dozen Rolex watches color-coordinated to match Jose "Coca-Cola" Yero's wardrobe, and various houses in Dade and Palm Beach counties, a search of one of which turns up not just a photograph of Jose "Coca-Cola" Yero face down in a pile of white powder but also a framed poster of Al Pacino as Tony Montana, the Mariel who appears at a dramatic moment in *Scarface* face down in a pile of white powder. "They got swept up in the fast lane," a Metro-Dade narcotics detective advises the *Herald*. "The fast lane is what put this whole group in jail." A young woman in South Palm Beach goes out to the parking lot of her parents' condominium and gets into her 1979 Pontiac Firebird, opens the T-top, starts the ignition and loses four toes when the bomb goes off. "She definitely knows someone is trying to kill her," the sheriff's investigator tells the *Herald*. "She knew they were coming, but she didn't know when."

Surfaces tended to dissolve here. Clear days ended less so. I recall an October Sunday when my husband and I were taken, by Gene Miller, a *Herald* editor who had won two Pulitzer Prizes for investigative reporting and who had access to season tickets exactly on the fifty-yard line at the Orange Bowl, to see the Miami Dolphins beat the Pittsburgh Steelers, 21–17. In the row below us the former Dolphin quarterback Earl Morrall signed autographs for the children who wriggled over seats to slip him their programs and steal surreptitious glances at his Super Bowl ring. A few rows back an Anglo teenager in sandals and shorts and a black T-shirt smoked a marijuana cigarette in full view of the Hispanic police officer behind him. Hot dogs were passed, and Coca-Cola spilled. Sony Watchmans were compared, for the definition on the instant replay. The NBC cameras dollied along the sidelines and the Dolphin cheerleaders kneeled on their white pom-poms and there was a good deal of talk about red dogging and weak secondaries and who would be seen and what would be eaten in New Orleans, come Super Bowl weekend.

The Miami on display in the Orange Bowl that Sunday afternoon would have seemed another Miami altogether, one with less weather and harder, more American surfaces, but by dinner we were slipping back into the tropical: in a virtually empty restaurant on top of a virtually empty condominium off Biscayne Boulevard, with six people at the table, one of whom was Gene Miller and one of whom was Martin Dardis, who as the chief investigator for the state attorney's office in Miami had led Carl Bernstein through the local angles on Watergate and who remained a walking data bank on CDs at the Biscayne Bank and on who called who on what payoff and on how to follow a money chain, we sat and we talked and we watched a storm break over Biscayne Bay. Sheets of warm rain washed down the big windows. Lightning began to fork somewhere around Bal Harbour. Gene Miller mentioned the Alberto Duque trial, then entering its fourth week at the federal courthouse, the biggest bank fraud case ever tried in the United States. Martin Dardis mentioned the ESM Government Securities collapse, just then breaking into a fraud case maybe bigger than the Duque.

The lightning was no longer forking now but illuminating the entire sky, flashing a dead strobe white, turning the bay fluorescent and the islands black, as if in negative. I sat and I listened to Gene Miller and Martin Dardis discuss these old and new turns in the underwater narrative and I watched the lightning backlight the islands. During the time I had spent in Miami many people had mentioned, always as something extraordinary, something I should have seen if I wanted to understand Miami, the *Surrounded Islands* project executed in Biscayne Bay in 1983 by the Bulgarian artist Christo. *Surrounded Islands*, which had involved surrounding eleven islands with two-hundred-foot petals, or skirts, of pink polypropylene fabric, had been mentioned both by people who were knowledgeable about conceptual art and by people who had not before heard and could not then recall the name of the man who had surrounded the islands. All had agreed. It seemed that the pink had shimmered in the water. It seemed that the pink had kept changing color, fading and reemerging with the movement of the water and the clouds and the sun and the night lights. It seemed that this period when the pink was in the water had for many people exactly defined, as the backlit islands and the fluorescent water and the voices at the table were that night defining for me, Miami.

Questions for Critical Thinking and Writing

1. How does Didion carry the metaphor of water and liquid throughout the essay? What is she using the "drought" to signify in Miami?

2. What does Didion mean by the phrase, "Nothing about Miami was exactly fixed, or hard," and what anecdotes does she use to support this statement?

3. In the closing paragraph, Didion describes a modern art piece that she says was "that night defining for me, Miami." How does the art reflect her view of Miami, and why might she have chosen to end the essay with that image?

Nathaniel Hawthorne

Best known for his short stories and his novel *The Scarlet Letter* (1850), Nathaniel Hawthorne (1804–1864) was an American writer from Salem, Massachusetts. He graduated from Bowdoin College in 1825, having made acquaintances like the poet Henry Wadsworth Longfellow. He had great reverence for beauty in all forms and wrote in his short story "The Marble Faun," "Nobody, I think, ought to read poetry, or look at pictures or statues, who cannot find a great deal more in them than the poet or artist has actually expressed."

Courtesy of Time & Life Pictures/Getty Images.

Nathaniel Hawthorne

BEFORE YOU READ

Ponce de León's search for the fountain of youth fascinated Nathaniel Hawthorne. As you read, think about the value of youth versus the value of
age—what lesson does Hawthorne's story aim to teach in regard to eternal
youth?

Ponce de León's Fountain of Youth   1850

"Did you never hear of the fountain of youth?" he inquired of his guests,
"which Ponce de León, the Spanish adventurer, went in search of?"

"Did Ponce de León ever find it?" asked the Widow Wycherly.

"No," answered Dr. Heidegger, "for he never sought for it in the right
place. The famous Fountain of Youth is situated in the southern part of the
peninsula of Florida. Its source is overshadowed by several gigantic magnolias,
which, though numberless centuries old, have been kept fresh as violets by the
virtues of this wonderful water. An acquaintance of mine, knowing my curios-
ity in such matters, has sent me some of it which you see in this vase. All of
you, my respected friends, are welcome to as much of this admirable fluid as
may restore you to the bloom of youth. For my own part having had so much
trouble in growing old, I am in no hurry to grow young again."

He accordingly proceeds to administer to his four aged friends several
draughts of the water; which restore them, first to advanced middle age, then
to the prime of life, and lastly to the first glow and vigour of early youth.
Instantly they begin to display all the vanities and follies they had practiced
sixty years before. The three gentlemen dispute and quarrel, first angrily and
then furiously, for the favour of the lady. She practices all the coquetry of her
girlhood, inciting to a still higher pitch the passions of her suitors, until in
their struggles they overthrow the vase, and spill the water. This, it is found,
is very transient in its effects. The four rejuvenescents soon begin to grow old
again, and clamorously entreat the doctor to procure some more of the wonderful water; failing which they resolve straightaway to set out for Florida, and
quaff morning, noon and night, of the Fountain of Youth. The doctor's final
remarks are too fine to be omitted.

"So, the Water of Youth is all lavished on the ground. Well, I bemoan it
not, for if the fountain gushed at my door step, I would not stoop to bathe
my lips in it—no, not though its delirium were for years instead of moments!
Such is the lesson ye have taught me!"

QUESTIONS FOR CRITICAL THINKING AND WRITING

1. Why does Dr. Heidegger have no interest in trying the water at the beginning of the story? Does he change his mind at the end?

2. What happens to the guests after they have tried the water from the fountain of youth? How does their reaction affect Dr. Heidegger?

3. Analyze the doctor's final remarks—why does he not bemoan the spilled
   water, and what does he mean by the "delirium" caused by the water?

ANNE E. ROWE

A biographical note for Anne E. Rowe appears on page 8.

BEFORE YOU READ

The following essay is an example of literary criticism, and it focuses on Ernest Hemingway's novel *To Have and Have Not* (an excerpt from that book appears on p. 70). As you read, think about the merits of analyzing literature as a way to learn about a culture. What might you be able to learn from Hemingway's protagonist Harry Morgan that you would not learn in a nonfiction historical text?

The Last Wild Country   1986

The launch rolled in the Gulf Stream swell and Harry Morgan lay
on his back in the cockpit. At first he tried to brace himself against
the roll with his good hand. Then he lay quietly and took it.
            —Ernest Hemingway, *To Have and Have Not*

In April of 1928 a young writer returning from his years as an expatriate in Europe arrived by ship in Key West harbor. Ernest Hemingway, already renowned for his fiction, had come with his new wife, Pauline Pfeiffer, for what was to be a stay of six weeks or so before deciding upon a place of residence in America. It took only a few days of exploring the town, its beaches, its bars, its opportunities for deep sea fishing, to capture Hemingway's admiration for the place. Key West was remotely situated sixty miles from mainland Florida, and its population had dwindled to only twelve thousand from the boom times of the mid-twenties. The planned visit of a few weeks led to a number of lengthy stays and finally to the purchase of a house where Hemingway did some of his best writing. Key West was to become the setting for *To Have and Have Not*, his only novel based in America. When Hemingway finally made a complete break from Key West in 1940, it was to move one hundred miles south to Cuba in hopes of regaining those very things that had appealed to him in Key West.

For what Hemingway found in Florida was a wild, tropical place that was still largely unfettered by the entrapments of civilized everyday life. Hemingway's Florida was a place where a man could match himself against the elements in contests with the great marlin, a place where someone daring enough could run whiskey for handsome profits. In this Florida one could find the freedom largely lacking in the rest of the country, the freedom to live and thrive according to the tenets of one's own code. Only in the 1930s, when the government in the form of the Works Progress Administration and other projects began to interfere with Florida as he knew it, did Hemingway strike out for new territory.

The appeal of Key West to Hemingway's imagination is understandable. Given its relative isolation, the cosmopolitan qualities of Key West were remarkable. As one chronicler of the town notes: "The history of Key West dates back to Indians, Spanish explorers, conquistadors, and pirates. Because of its strategic location, the island became a melting pot. Lighthearted Cubans mingled with Bahamian seamen. New England sea captains, merchants, and aristocratic southerners rubbed elbows to create a unique island culture."[1]

Key West had reached its boom period after the completion of Henry Flagler's overseas railroad in 1912 when the population grew to almost twenty thousand. The town continued to thrive as a military center during World War I. With the end of the war, Key West suffered a number of economic losses: "the armed forces were moved away; the cigar factories had departed to Tampa and sponge fishing was taken over by the divers from Tarpon Springs."[2]

When Hemingway arrived in Key West the town had not yet plunged to its economic depths. After the collapse of the Florida boom and the onset of the depression, a number of residents moved away. By 1933 a fourth of the population was on relief, and the following year the community was placed in the hands of the Federal Emergency Relief Administration, which planned to rebuild the town into a resort. Volunteers, including artists who created murals on buildings throughout the town, worked to refurbish Key West into a tourist center, but a major setback occurred when the hurricane of September, 1935, destroyed parts of the overseas railroad and killed almost five hundred war veterans who lived in three Civilian Conservation Corps camps on the Keys. Hemingway was among those who searched for bodies, and believing, as did many others, that the veterans' deaths could have been avoided by more efficient warnings of the impending hurricane, he wrote a scathing article, "The Three-Day Blow," protesting their deaths.

Key West did not begin to thrive in an economic way again until the Overseas Highway, built in part on the remaining railroad pilings, was completed in 1938, opening the town again as a tourist center. As James McLendon has noted, "Even before the 1935 hurricane the New Deal was heavily committed to the Keys." The government "meant to rebuild them; they meant to help the people and they did. But to the hardy Conchs and to artists like Hemingway the changes would be hard to accept." With the completion of the Overseas Highway and the building of federal housing projects, "the island charm was on the wane. Middle-class America was on its way to Key West after more than a hundred years."[3] And for Hemingway it was time to light out for the territory again.

How Hemingway made his way to Key West has been amply documented. Probably no other American writer has had his life so thoroughly explored and written about as has Hemingway. Not only have the details of his life spawned a cult of hero-worshipers, but the biographical fallacies have become a major obstacle to the interpretation of his work. As Louis D. Rubin, Jr., has noted, "Once we are familiar with Hemingway, we tend to regard all of his fiction as extensions of his personality."[4] What is important here is to determine what drew Hemingway to Key West and how he used both the setting and the protagonist, Harry Morgan of *To Have and Have Not*, to tell a story about Florida—and America.

To trace Hemingway's career before he settled in Key West and wrote *To Have and Have Not* is to realize some striking parallels with his fellow writers who preceded him to Florida. The similarities with Ring Lardner have been noted — growing up in a small midwestern town, striking out at a young age into a writing career. Philip Young has also pointed out the parallels with Stephen Crane. They both "began very young their careers as reporters, and quickly became foreign correspondents. They traveled widely, and to the same places: Key West, the American West and Cuba; Europe, a Greco-Turkish War, and so on." Although Hemingway later repudiated Lardner's influence, he acknowledged his indebtedness to Crane, seeing in "The Open Boat" Crane's concern with style and with the relationship between man and his environment.[5]

Although they seem an unlikely pair for comparison, Hemingway and Henry James also share similar qualities. Hugh Holman notes that Hemingway "is most like James for he left America without leaving Americans; in large measure he deserted the American scene in his major works . . . but he made his subject in part the American abroad." Holman also notes the two share a "single-minded devotion to . . . craft."[6] Most important for this study, however, is the fact that both writers, returning to America from Europe, found in Florida what they would use symbolically as the heart and soul of America. For James six days in Florida was sufficient; in contrast, Hemingway's visit to Florida turned into a stay of some twelve years.

Hemingway had already conquered Europe, married, divorced, and married a second time before he returned to America in 1928. In Key West he and his second wife, Pauline, rented an apartment. The colorful setting and history of Key West, which lies approximately 120 miles out to sea, only 90 miles from Cuba and 150 miles away from the Bahamas, instantly appealed to him. When Hemingway arrived, Key West had been linked to the mainland by Henry Flagler's railroad for only sixteen years. The Overseas Highway would not be built for some years.

In his study of Hemingway's years in Key West, James McLendon argues that "the single most important chunk of the author's life has been passed over and almost obscured to date." Referring to the twelve years from 1928 to 1940 that Hemingway spent as a "permanent or sometime resident," McLendon says that in the "strange cosmopolitan backwater" of Key West, "with its almost mystical island presence, he found what he was to become." Dos Passos, who visited Hemingway several times, was also to sense the faraway quality of the place that he described as "something seen in a dream."[7]

Alfred Kazin has also commented on the special qualities of Hemingway's newfound home.

> Like the Paris of 1925, Key West is at once an outpost of a culture and its symbol. It is a home for disabled and unemployed veterans, a night resort for writers who talk great books, a harbor for the sleek yachts of the newer millionaires. Being a tip of the continent, it is an open door to Cuba, a window on the Gulf Stream, the Florida of the boom all over again, albeit a little tarnished; and a bit of Latin America. It is by Key West that Hemingway went home, and it is Key West, apparently, that remains America in cross-section to him; the noisy, shabby, deeply moving rancor and tumult of all those human wrecks, the fishermen and the Cuban revolutionaries, the veterans and the alcoholics, the gilt-edged snobs and the hungry natives, the great white stretch of beach promising everything and leading nowhere.[8]

After several moves, Hemingway and Pauline established a permanent home on Whitehead Street. They restored a large, run-down house, built the first swimming pool in Key West, and equipped a study for the writer on the second floor of the old carriage house. Hemingway was not amused when the Whitehead Street house was designated as stop number eighteen on a list prepared by the tourist board of forty-eight things to see in Key West. One of his favorite stories was that he kept an aged black man out front to impersonate him and run off tourists.[9] If he was frustrated by the affronts to his privacy, he continued to be taken with the charms of the town, and later, when he felt Key West was growing too large, he nevertheless could effectively describe the lure of its surroundings.

> In the first place, the Gulf Stream and the other great ocean currents are the last wild country there is left. Once you are out of sight of land and of the other boats you are more alone than you can ever be hunting and the sea is the same as it has been since before men ever went on it in boats. In a season fishing you will see it oily flat as the becalmed galleons saw it while they drifted to the westward; white-capped with a fresh breeze as they saw it running with the trades. . . . The Gulf Stream is an unexploited country.[10]

Ernest Hemingway's home in Key West, 1933. After returning from Paris, Hemingway settled in Key West. His home is now one of the city's most famous literary landmarks.
Wright Langley.

Four boys dancing in front of the Hemingway residence in Key West, 1939.
Courtesy of the State Archives of Florida.

Key West meant many things to Hemingway. Although it was far from an urban center, its cosmopolitan qualities appealed to the recent expatriate. At the same time its relative isolation from the mainstream of life afforded him the privacy necessary for his work. When he finished his daily writing stint, there were plenty of pleasures to indulge in — swimming with friends, drinking at Sloppy Joe's Bar, fishing in the Gulf all the way to Cuba.

More important than these things, Key West sparked Hemingway's imagination. As Kazin has noted, Key West, in many ways, represented the best and worst in America. On one hand Key West with its juxtaposition of down-and-out veterans and poor fishermen with wealthy yacht owners showed America of the thirties — the depression years when the great contrasts between the haves and have-nots were accentuated. In Key West there were natives, known as Conchs, who could hardly make enough money to feed their families. Only a few hundred yards away in their yachts in the harbor were the idle rich that Lardner had poked fun at in his stories. When Hemingway came to write about the latter group of people he would, as Lardner had done, show them desperately seeking happiness and rarely finding it.

But if Key West showed the misery of the thirties, it nevertheless retained many of the paradisic qualities that had drawn so many people to it in the first place. The temperate climate, beautiful ocean vistas, and most important to Hemingway, the lawlessness, including smuggling tax-free rum even after Prohibition had ended, that prevailed there were highly appealing. Key West natives had their own standards of government, and because of its remote location, there was in Hemingway's time (and still to a great degree today) a primitive, frontier quality to the place. Hemingway had referred to the Gulf

Stream as an unspoiled place; to a large extent, Key West was still a place where a man could live by his own code and people would not trouble him about it.

Although Hemingway treated the Keys in several magazine articles and one story, his most sustained treatment came in the book that was to arouse much controversy, *To Have and Have Not*. Probably the harshest criticism of the novel was that of Delmore Schwartz. "*To Have and Have Not* is a stupid and foolish book, a disgrace to a good writer, a book which should never have been printed." A more balanced assessment is Alfred Kazin's review in which he found the novel "feverishly brilliant, and flat by turns."[11]

To determine what Hemingway did well in *To Have and Have Not* it is necessary first to consider what he did wrong. As Carlos Baker observed, "Hemingway himself once described [the novel] . . . as a procedural error—an attempt, that is, to make a novel out of what ought to have remained a novelette about a Key West soldier of fortune named Harry Morgan." Instead of doing this, Hemingway worked off and on at the book for three or four years. The Morgan episodes were "first conceived and first written as three short stories." The first, "One Trip Across," published in 1934, introduces Harry Morgan, "ex-policeman from Miami, charter-boat fisherman out of Key West, a proud and independent man who took to smuggling as a means of supporting his wife and daughters in lieu of letting them go on relief." The second Harry Morgan story, written in 1935 and entitled "The Tradesman's Return," has Harry losing his right arm to gunfire and having his boat confiscated after bringing over illegal liquor from Cuba. Hemingway, as Baker notes, had decided to flesh out these stories into a novel. Taking the material with him to Wyoming, he worked on a third Morgan story and a companion story in which he introduced the young Richard Gordon, a failed writer, and his friends. Richard Gordon, his wife, and the smart social set were to be used as a foil for the simple, hardworking Harry Morgan and his blowsy but loving wife, Marie, a former prostitute.[12]

It is an overstatement to say, as did one critic, that the only unity in *To Have and Have Not* is in the binding, but certainly Hemingway's plan for the book, which looked good on paper, did not work out.[13] The final result is an awkward yoking together of segments: there is the Harry Morgan story, the central plot of the book; the Richard Gordon story, with its sneering comments on the failed writer who looks for "quaintness" in faraway Key West and misunderstands everything he sees; and finally there is the roll call of the yachts at the conclusion of the novel in which Hemingway condemns the empty life of the rich—the homosexual rich boy who will soon commit suicide, the nymphomaniac woman whose lover ignores her, and so on.

As Baker notes in his able analysis of *To Have and Have Not*: "The assumption in [the novel] was that Depressed America at large could be anatomized by using a microscope on Key West in little. America at its worst was fully visible in Key West during the period 1932–36." A noble plan, but artistically one that, for Hemingway at least, simply did not work. The story of Richard Gordon, meant to heighten the Harry Morgan story and to throw "Harry Morgan's masculine virtue into bolder relief," generally adds nothing to the Morgan story.[14] Additionally, the long concluding section on the yachts with its shifts in point of view from the have nots to the haves contains some of Hemingway's blandest writing. The wealthy people on the boats are merely caricatures of people; they are so cardboardlike that they fail to sustain the reader's interest. If *To Have and Have Not* was one of Hemingway's rare attempts, as some critics have said, to write a novel of social protest, it failed both thematically (the message was undercut by the weakness of the characters he was using to illustrate his points) and artistically (the juxtaposition of the thesis material distorted what was in itself an exciting, well-fashioned story—the tale of Harry Morgan).

Almost all of what does succeed in *To Have and Have Not*, then, is related to the story of Morgan's life and death struggles. Harry's story grows out of that other aspect of Key West that Hemingway found there—the last frontier, a place where there was still room for heroes.

As with almost every aspect of *To Have and Have Not*, a critical controversy has continued over whether Harry Morgan is hero or villain; is he a man who does the wrong things for the right reasons, or is he a murderous, evil renegade? This much seems clear: from the outset of the story Harry Morgan is a doomed man, betrayed by the social and economic conditions of his life.

We are first introduced to Morgan in a bar in Havana where after turning down a handsome offer of money for smuggling Cubans to the Keys, he sees them gunned down on the sidewalk outside the cafe. Harry has said that he does not like to smuggle anything that can talk. Returning to his boat, Harry takes Mr. Johnson, a wealthy businessman from the States, out on the final day of three weeks of fishing. Morgan's analysis of Johnson is an unflattering one. Johnson loses a marlin that "a fisherman would give a year to tie into . . . he loses my heavy tackle, he makes a fool of himself and he sits there perfectly content, drinking with a rummy" (*THHN*, 22).[15] If Johnson is a fool, he is also morally corrupt; for after promising to pay Harry the $825 he owes him on the next day, he takes a plane to Miami. Morgan and his mate, Eddy the rummy, are left in Havana with not even enough money to buy fuel for the trip back to Key West.

Only because Harry is without money does he then strike a deal with a Chinaman, Mr. Sing, to transport a dozen Chinese to the Keys. Assured by Sing that it does not matter where he drops them and knowing that Sing, a broker, wants only the money and has no concern for the lives of the refugees, Harry accepts the money, then after the Chinese are transferred to his boat, kills Sing and dumps the Chinese back on shore. His justification for this act is that he killed Sing "to keep from killing twelve other Chinese" (*THHN*, 55). He returns to Key West with $1200, enough to support Marie and their daughters for the summer.

In Part Two of the novel Harry is smuggling liquor up to the Keys because "the depression had put charter boat fishing on the bum" (*THHN*, 85). When he and his black mate Wesley are pursued and Wesley is shot in the leg and Harry wounded in the arm, Harry pulls the boat up close to shore on one of the outer Keys, and with his one good arm begins to toss the liquor overboard. In this scene the Key West code is clearly apparent. Another fisherman, Captain Willie, who has chartered his boat to a party of visitors, sees Morgan's boat. When his party tells Captain Willie to go alongside, he refuses. "If he wanted us he would have signalled us. If he don't want us it's none of our business. Down here everybody aims to mind their own business" (*THHN*, 79). The visitor, Frederick Harrison, tells the captain that he is "one of the three most important men in the United States today" and orders Willie to approach the boat, to which the captain responds, asking him if he is so important, "What the hell you doing in Key West, then?" The captain then calls out to Harry, "I got a guy here on board some kind of stool from Washington. More important than the President, he says. . . . He thinks you're a bootlegger. He's got the numbers of the boat. I ain't never seen you so I don't know who you are. . . . I don't know where this place is where I seen you. I wouldn't know how to get back here" (*THHN*, 80, 83).

Like Johnson, Harrison is another outsider, a violator of the code. Another indication of his inability to appreciate the value of Key West is found in his remark, "Fishing is nonsense. . . . If you catch a sailfish what do you do with it?" (*THHN*, 82). Harrison has no understanding of the importance of the ritual that takes place in the struggle, just as he has no appreciation of the code of life Hemingway is writing about.

As Part Two closes, Harry, having lost his liquor and fearing that his boat will be confiscated by the Coast Guard, worries about his wound. "I hope they can fix that arm. . . . I got a lot of use for that arm" (*THHN*, 87). In the beginning of Part Three, Harry, now one-armed, is in Freddy's Bar making arrangements to smuggle some Cuban revolutionaries back to Havana. His confiscated boat is tied up in the harbor, but he plans to steal it. He enlists the help of Albert, a friend of his who is now working on relief earning $7.50 a week digging up sewer lines. Harry's sermon to Al sums up the economic situation in Key West and justifies Harry's illegal smuggling activities. "Look at me. I used to make thirty-five dollars a day right through the season taking people out fishing. Now I get shot and lose an arm, and my boat, running a lousy load of liquor that's worth hardly as much as my boat. But let me tell you, my kids ain't going to have their bellies hurt and I ain't going to dig sewers for the government for less money than will feed them. . . . they're trying to . . . starve you Conchs out of here so they can burn down the shacks and put up apartments and make this a tourist town. . . . they're buying up lots, and then after the poor people are starved out and gone somewhere else to starve some more they're going to come in and make it into a beauty spot for tourists" (*THHN*, 96).

Albert, who is the narrator of this section of Part Three, reflects on Harry. "When he was in a boat he always felt good and without his boat he felt plenty bad. I think he was glad of an excuse to steal her" (*THHN*, 97). Although Harry rescues his boat, its hiding place is discovered, and desperate to earn some money, he hires the *Queen Conch* owned by Freddy but does not tell him the real reason for using it. Having rendezvoused with the revolutionaries after they have robbed a bank to finance their revolutionary activities, he soon realizes the full extent of the danger he is in. In these final scenes Harry's (and perhaps Hemingway's) ambivalence about the revolution is reflected. The Cubans kill Albert so that he cannot talk, and one of the Cubans explains to Harry that Albert's murderer "is a good revolutionary but a bad man. . . . He kills in a good cause, of course. The best cause" (*THHN*, 158). Harry muses to himself, "To help the working man he robs a bank and kills a fellow works with him and then kills that poor damned Albert that never did any harm. That's a working man he kills" (*THHN*, 168).

Harry knows he must kill the Cubans before they murder him. "He had abandoned anger, hatred and any dignity as luxuries, now, and had started to plan" (*THHN*, 159). He shoots the Cubans, but one of them wounds him in the stomach. In the final scene with Harry, the Coast Guard tows in the *Queen Conch* and a crowd gathers in the harbor to see it brought in. "The crowd was as quiet as only a Key West crowd can be" (*THHN*, 227). At the conclusion of the novel, Marie, grieving for the loss of her husband, returns home, and in a book in which there is remarkably little description of the lush surroundings, the author leaves the reader with this little coda after Morgan's death: "Outside it was a lovely, cool, sub-tropical winter day and the palm branches were sawing in the light north wind. . . . In the big yard of the house across the street a peacock squawked. Through the window you could see the sea looking hard and new and blue in the winter light" (*THHN*, 261–62). Here the wildness and freedom and beauty of Key West are figured as an appropriate setting for the life and death of Harry Morgan.

For those critics who see *To Have and Have Not* as a complete failure, the death of Harry Morgan is nothing more than the sordid end of a smuggler. But as Baker and others have noted, Harry Morgan's life can be seen as much more. Given the context of his setting and his faithful adherence to his own code of ethics, Harry Morgan is a tragic hero.

Both Leo Gurko and Philip Young have not missed the point that Harry's namesake was Henry Morgan, "the pirate, who once ravaged the coasts off which Harry works, who like Harry was really hard, but brave and resourceful too." As Young accurately observes, "Where the parallel breaks down, we get what may be the main point of it; following his capture by the law Henry was knighted; Harry was killed."[16]

Not only did Hemingway provide Harry with a special antecedent; it is not difficult to see Harry as "a lineal descendent of the American frontiersman, the man who made his own laws and trusted in his own judgments. . . . Both in the Far West and in Key West Hemingway had met men of the frontier temperament, so that he did not lack for contemporary models." Baker concludes, "there is no difficulty in taking Morgan as the type of the old, self-reliant individualist confronted by an ever-encroaching social restraint."[17] For restraint is precisely what Harry Morgan encounters, as Richard Lehan notes. "Hemingway explicitly contrasts the elemental man with a sick society that destroys him, and this novel is Hemingway's most expressed attack on America and modern culture."[18] Unlike his predecessors who could always move on, time and place had run out for Harry. "Huck Finn could always light out for the territory when things got too uncomfortable at home. In Harry Morgan's time there was no territory to light out for. He managed to escape from the settled, overcrowded earth to water, but even the free expanse of water was no longer free. Every country in the Caribbean had coast-guard cutters, chopping up the sea in controllable segments, boxing in those who sought to maneuver on their own."[19] Betrayed by capitalists, and governments, Harry has no chance for victory, except perhaps in death. And in typical Hemingway fashion, he accepts death stoically. To the people on the yachts who witness Harry's boat being towed in he is nothing but another dead Conch, but to the perceptive reader Harry Morgan, through his adherence to the code of individuality, has lived by it and died by it, nobly.

Harry Morgan was squeezed out of his paradise at last by the encroachment of institutions and people. But in his depiction of Harry, Hemingway portrayed some of Key West's finest elements. For a time at least Key West was one of the few outposts in America where the frontier spirit survived.

Like Harry Morgan, Hemingway loved the individualistic spirit of Key West. The breakup of his second marriage and the building of the Overseas Highway to the Keys were both factors in bringing an end to his enjoyment of the easy pace of life there. With Key West closed to him, he would turn to Cuba, the Bahamas, and the Gulf Stream itself for the final works, *The Old Man and the Sea* and the posthumously published *Islands in the Stream*. But the Key West interlude had been an important one for Hemingway. He did some of his best writing there (*A Farewell to Arms*) and though *To Have and Have Not* falls short of being one of his best works, the character of Harry Morgan epitomized perhaps one of the last American heroes who could still live, for a time at least, by an individualistic, primitive code.

As Leo Gurko has noted, during the time Hemingway was in Key West the depression "toppled the businessman as the reigning god in the American pantheon and substituted the idea of collective action for the early pioneer idea of individual free enterprise. But at the height of the depression there was a period when the old order was cracking up while the new one was not yet in sight."[20] Key West reflected this change, even though some individuals resisted it. Harry Morgan scrambled to live by his own individualistic code even as the effects of the depression robbed him of his livelihood, and finally his life.

In his portrayal of Florida in *To Have and Have Not*, Hemingway showed what had seemed a paradise, a holdout against bourgeois American life, at the very moment when it would have to succumb, to a degree at least, to the forces of the depression that were controlling the rest of America. And it is precisely because this southern outpost of Florida was being threatened that its primitive qualities remained so important in Hemingway's vision. This wild, primitive place, so isolated that it maintained its own individualistic code into the early decades of the twentieth-century industrial age, remained for Hemingway the heart of what America had once been and had now lost. Although fast disappearing, it was the last wild country.

NOTES

1. Jim Brasher, "Hemingway's Florida," *Lost Generation Journal*, I (1973), 4.
2. J. E. Dovell, *Florida: Historic, Dramatic, Contemporary*, II (New York, 1952), 810.
3. James McLendon, *Papa: Hemingway in Key West* (Miami, Fla., 1972), 138-39.
4. Louis D. Rubin, Jr., "The Self Recaptured," *Kenyon Review*, XXV (1963), 412.
5. Philip Young, *Ernest Hemingway* (New York, 1952), 162, 164.
6. C. Hugh Holman, "Ernest Hemingway," in "Modern Novelists and Contemporary American Society: A Symposium," *Shenandoah*, X (Winter, 1959), 5.
7. McLendon, *Papa*, 16, 20.
8. Alfred Kazin, "Hemingway's First Book on His Own People," in Robert O. Stephens (ed.), *Ernest Hemingway: The Critical Reception* (New York, 1977), 175.
9. Ernest Hemingway, "The Sights of Whitehead Street: A Key West Letter," in William White (ed.), *By-Line: Ernest Hemingway: Selected Articles and Dispatches of Four Decades* (New York, 1967), 192.
10. Ernest Hemingway, "On the Blue Water: A Gulf Stream Letter," in White (ed.), *By-Line*, 237-38.
11. Delmore Schwartz, "Ernest Hemingway's Literary Situation," in John K. M. McCaffery (ed.), *Ernest Hemingway: The Man and His Work* (New York, 1969), 123; Kazin, "Hemingway's First Book on His Own People," in Stephens (ed.), *Ernest Hemingway: The Critical Reception*, 174.
12. Carlos Baker, *Hemingway: The Writer as Artist* (4th ed.; Princeton, 1972), xv-xvi, 203-04.

13. William James Ryan, "Uses of Irony in *To Have and Have Not*," *Modern Fiction Studies*, XIV (Autumn, 1968), 329.

14. Baker, *Hemingway: The Writer as Artist*, 206, 204–05.

15. Ernest Hemingway, *To Have and Have Not* (New York: Simon and Schuster, 1937).

16. Young, *Ernest Hemingway*, 43–44. See also Leo Gurko, *Ernest Hemingway and the Pursuit of Heroism* (New York, 1968), 149.

17. Baker, *Hemingway: The Writer as Artist*, 210–11.

18. Richard Lehan, "Hemingway Among the Moderns," in Richard Astro and Jackson J. Benson (eds.), *Hemingway in Our Time* (Corvallis, 1974), 202.

19. Gurko, *Ernest Hemingway and the Pursuit of Heroism*, 148.

20. Ibid., 143.

QUESTIONS FOR CRITICAL THINKING AND WRITING

1. What qualities does Rowe argue Hemingway shares with Henry James? How are these reflected in Hemingway's work set in Florida?

2. Rowe argues that Hemingway used Florida not only as a setting but also as a representation of America as a whole. How did Key West "represent . . . the best and worst in America"?

3. What is the significance of the title of the essay, and how does it describe the content of *To Have and Have Not*?

ERNEST HEMINGWAY

Ernest Hemingway (1899–1961) was born in Illinois, and after serving in World War I, relocated to France, where he was a member of a highly lauded expatriate group of writers. When he returned from Paris, he settled in Key West, Florida, the setting for *To Have and Have Not*, from which the following story is excerpted. Best known for his novels, Courtesy of John Van Hasselt/Sygma/Corbis. including *The Sun Also Rises* (1926), *A Farewell to Arms* (1929), and *For Whom the Bell Tolls* (1940), and the novella *The Old Man and the Sea* (1952), Hemingway was also a journalist and reporter for Canadian and American newspapers. In 1954 he won the Nobel Prize in literature.

BEFORE YOU READ

As you read this excerpt from *To Have and Have Not*, pay attention to the effectiveness of the language and the different elements of the story. As a reader, do you find this passage successful? Does it make you want to read on? Why or why not?

From *To Have and Have Not*

Freddy Wallace's boat, the *Queen Conch*, 34 feet long, with a V number out of Tampa, was painted white; the forward deck was painted a color called Frolic green and the inside of the cockpit was painted Frolic green. The top of the house was painted the same color. Her name and home port, Key West, Fla., were painted in black across her stern. She was not equipped with out-riggers and had no mast. She was equipped with glass windshields, one of which, that forward of the wheel, was broken. There were a number of fresh, wood-splintered holes in the newly painted planking of her hull. Splintered patches could be seen on both sides of her hull about a foot below the gunwale and a little forward of the center of the cockpit. There was another group of these splintered places almost at the water line on the starboard side of the hull opposite the aft stanchion that supported her house or awning. From the lower of these holes something dark had dripped and hung in ropy lines against the new paint of her hull.

She drifted broadside to the gentle north wind about ten miles outside of the north-bound tanker lanes, gay looking in her fresh white and green, against the dark, blue Gulf Stream water. There were patches of sun-yellowed Sargasso weed floating in the water near her that passed her slowly in the current going to the north and east, while the wind overcame some of the launch's drift as it set her steadily further out into the stream. There was no sign of life on her although the body of a man showed, rather inflated looking, above the gunwale, lying on a bench over the port gasoline tank and, from the long seat alongside the starboard gunwale, a man seemed to be leaning over to dip his hand into the sea. His head and arms were in the sun and at the point where his fingers almost touched the water, there was a school of small fish, about two inches long, oval-shaped, golden-colored, with faint purple stripes, that had deserted the gulf weed to take shelter in the shade the bottom of the drifting launch made in the water, and each time anything dripped down into the sea, these fish rushed at the drop and pushed and milled until it was gone. Two gray sucker fish about eighteen inches long swam round and round the boat in the shadow in the water, their slit mouths on the tops of their flat heads opening and shutting; but they did not seem to comprehend the regu-larity of the drip the small fish fed on and were as likely to be on the far side of the launch when the drop fell as near it. They had long since pulled away the ropy, carmine clots and threads that trailed in the water from the lowest splintered holes, shaking their ugly, sucker-topped heads and their elongated, tapering, thin-tailed bodies as they pulled. They were reluctant now to leave a place where they had fed so well and unexpectedly.

Inside the cockpit of the launch there were three other men. One, dead, lay on his back where he had fallen below the steering stool. Another, dead, lay humped big against the scupper by the starboard aft stanchion. The third, still alive, but long out of his head, lay on his side with his head on his arm.

The bilge of the launch was full of gasoline and when she rolled at all this made a sloshing sound. The man, Harry Morgan, believed this sound was in his own belly and it seemed to him now that his belly was big as a lake and that it sloshed on both shores at once. That was because he was on his back now with his knees drawn up and his head back. The water of the lake that was his belly was very cold; so cold that when he stepped into its edge it numbed him, and he was extremely cold now and everything tasted of gasoline as though he had been sucking on a hose to syphon a tank. He knew there was no tank although he could feel a cold rubber hose that seemed to have entered his mouth and now was coiled, big, cold, and heavy all down through him. Each time he took a breath the hose coiled colder and firmer in his lower abdomen and he could feel it like a big, smooth-moving snake in there, above the sloshing of the lake. He was afraid of it, but although it was in him, it seemed a vast distance away and what he minded, now, was the cold.

The cold was all through him, an aching cold that would not numb away, and he lay quietly now and felt it. For a time he had thought that if he could pull himself up over himself it would warm him like a blanket, and he thought for a while that he had gotten himself pulled up and he had started to warm. But that warmth was really only the hemorrhage produced by raising his knees up; and as the warmth faded he knew now that you could not pull yourself up over yourself and there was nothing to do about the cold but take it. He lay there, trying hard in all of him not to die long after he could not think. He was in the shadow now, as the boat drifted, and it was colder all the time.

The launch had been drifting since 10 o'clock of the night before and it was now getting late in the afternoon. There was nothing else in sight across the surface of the Gulf Stream but the gulf weed, a few pink, inflated, membranous bubbles of Portuguese men-of-war cocked jauntily on the surface, and the distant smoke of a loaded tanker bound north from Tampico.

QUESTIONS FOR CRITICAL THINKING AND WRITING

1. How does Hemingway contrast the physical description of the boat and the water with the grim scene?

2. Read the short excerpt a second time. After knowing the outcome of the scene, do any of the details in the first paragraphs make more sense? What are those details, and how have they become clearer?

3. How would you describe the tone of this passage? How does the tone relate to the scene? Cite specific words or passages from the text to support your answer.

CARL HIAASEN

Carl Hiaasen, one of Florida's most acclaimed writers, was born in Florida in 1953 and has lived there for most of his life. After graduating from the University of Florida, he joined the *Miami Herald*, where, since 1985, he has penned a regular column for the paper. His writings have also appeared in numerous magazines, including *Sports Illustrated*, *Time*, *Esquire*, and *Gourmet*. Hiaasen has received many awards for his

Courtesy of Elena Selbert/Corbis.

nonfiction. In addition, he is the author of best-selling novels and popular books for children. The excerpt that follows is from his 2012 novel for young readers, *Chomp*. Read on, and you will find that it covers issues that people of any age can relate to.

Before You Read

Characters' interactions with one another can establish the tone and direction of a story. As you read this excerpt, pay close attention to the dialogue. How does it move the story forward? What does it say about each of the characters?

From *Chomp* 2012

Derek Badger's real name was Lee Bluepenny, and he had no training in biology, botany, geology, or forestry. His background was purely show business.

As a young man he'd traveled the world with a popular Irish folk-dancing group until he broke a toe while rehearsing for a street parade in Montreal. As he waited in the hospital emergency room, he happened to meet a talent agent who had gotten ill from eating tainted oysters. The queasy talent agent thought Lee Bluepenny looked tough and handsome, and asked if he'd ever considered a career in television.

As soon as Lee Bluepenny's dance injury healed, the agent arranged for him to fly to California and audition for a new reality show. The producers of *Expedition Survival!* loved Lee Bluepenny's new Australian accent, which he had shamelessly copied from the late Steve Irwin, the legendary crocodile hunter. The producers also liked that Lee Bluepenny could swallow a live salamander without throwing up. What they didn't particularly like was his name. Lee Bluepenny was okay for a jazz piano player or maybe an art dealer, they said, but it wasn't rugged-sounding enough for someone who had to claw and gnaw his way out of the wilds every week.

After trying out a few different names—Erik Panther, Gus Wolverine, Chad Condor—the producers settled on Derek Badger, which was fine with Lee Bluepenny. He was so thrilled to be on television that he would have let them call him Danny the Dodo Bird.

Expedition Survival! got off to a rocky start. The first episode was staged in a jungle in the Philippine Islands, where the man now called Derek Badger was supposed to be lost and starving. Disaster struck on the second day, when Derek was bitten severely by a striped shrew rat that he was attempting to gobble for dinner. The rodent had appeared to be dead, but it was only napping. Derek's punctured lips swelled up so badly from the bite that he looked like he was sucking on a football. A medical helicopter rushed him to Manila for rabies shots.

Eventually the rough spots in the show were smoothed out, and *Expedition Survival!* turned into a smash hit. It wasn't long before Derek Badger was an international celebrity, and he quickly learned to act like one.

"How's France?" Raven Stark asked when she called.

"Heaven," he said. "The cheese here is fantastic."

"I'm sure," said Raven Stark, with a note of concern. Survivalists were supposed to be lean and fit, and one of her main responsibilities was to keep Derek from getting too flabby. It wasn't easy—the man loved to eat, and cheese was high on his list.

"Did you find me a proper alligator?" he inquired.

"Yes, a beauty." She could hear him chewing and smacking his lips.

"How big?"

"Twelve feet," said Raven Stark.

"Brilliant!"

"And they've got a slightly smaller one you can tussle with."

There was a pause on the other end that made Raven Stark uneasy.

Derek said, "But I don't want to wrestle the small one. I want to wrestle the monster."

It was exactly the response she had feared. "Too dangerous," she said.

"Excuse me?"

"We can chat about this later, Derek."

"Indeed we will. What about a python? I told you I wanted a python."

"The gentleman has offered us a very large Burmese, though it's not tame."

"Even better!" chortled Derek.

Raven Stark sighed to herself. She was accustomed to working around Derek's enormous ego, but there were times when she felt like reminding him that he was basically a tap dancer, not a grizzled woodsman.

"Anything else that's super-scary?" he asked.

"I noticed they had a large snapping turtle," she said.

"How large?"

"Large enough to take off a hand."

"Excellent," Derek said. "Set up an underwater scene—I'm swimming along through the Everglades, minding my own business, when the hungry snapper charges out from under a log and drags me to the bottom of the lagoon."

"Right. Except turtles don't eat people."

"How do you know?" Derek demanded.

"Call me when you land in Miami," said Raven Stark.

Wahoo had an older sister named Julie who was finishing law school at the University of Florida in Gainesville. His father was secretly proud of her, but he wouldn't let on.

"Just what the world needs—another darn lawyer," he'd grumble.

"I love you, too, Dad," Julie would say, and pinch his cheek.

Wahoo thought his sister was pretty cool, although he sometimes felt intimidated because she was so smart and funny and sociable. Wahoo was shy, and not as self-confident. Julie had always been a straight-A student while Wahoo wasn't: his best-ever report card was two A's, four B's and a C (in algebra, naturally).

"Just do your best," his mom would say. "That's good enough for us."

Mickey Cray never really took an interest in the children's schoolwork because he was too busy with the animals.

"Put the old man on the phone," Julie said when she called.

"He's out working with the pythons," Wahoo reported.

"It's about the *Expedition* contract. I see problems."

Wahoo always faxed the TV contracts to his sister for her to see, even though his father normally signed them without reading a word.

"What's wrong, Jule?"

"Like, on page seven, it says the show 'shall have unrestricted use of the designated wildlife specimens for the duration of the production period.' That means they can do pretty much whatever they please with the animals—and they don't need to ask Pop's permission."

"This is bad," Wahoo said. He remembered what Raven Stark had said about Derek Badger wanting to wrestle one of the gators.

"Did the old man take any money yet?" Julie asked.

Wahoo told his sister about the eight-hundred-dollar deposit. She said Mickey could still get out of the deal if he returned the cash.

"Too late. He already spent it," said Wahoo.

"On what—monkey chow?"

"The mortgage."

"Ouch," said Wahoo's sister.

"We're sort of broke, Jule. Ever since he got hurt, it's been tough."

"So that's why Mom went to China. Now I get it."

Wahoo didn't want his sister to worry, so he tried to sound upbeat. "Pop's been doing way better since we took this job."

"Who is this Derek Badger character, anyway?"

"You've never seen the show?"

Julie chuckled. "I don't even own a TV, little bro. All I do up here is crack the books."

"Derek Badger is a survivalist guy," Wahoo said. He explained the adventure format of the program.

His sister said, "Give me a break."

"He's huge, Jule."

"Tell Dad what I said about the contract."

"Do I have to?" Wahoo said.

He was only half kidding. He knew it would be his problem soon enough.

Mickey Cray was barefoot in the backyard with Beulah the python. He was admiring the markings on her skin—rich, chocolate-colored saddles on a sleek silvery background. Fourteen feet of raw muscle, and a brain the size of a marble.

Ever since he was a boy, Mickey had kept snakes for pets—green tree snakes, king snakes, rat snakes, water snakes, ring-necked snakes, garter snakes, even a few poisonous rattlers and moccasins. Mickey had caught them all. He still found them fascinating and mysterious.

Now the Everglades was overrun with foreign pythons that were eating the deer, birds, rabbits, even alligators—it was really a rough scene. The pythons weren't supposed to be there; Southeast Asia was their natural home. So the U.S. government and the state of Florida had declared war on them.

Wahoo's father understood why: the snakes were totally disrupting the balance of nature. A single adult Burmese could lay more than fifty eggs at a time. They were among the largest predators in the world, growing to a length of twenty feet, and at that size had no natural enemies. Even panthers avoided them.

Because of his knowledge and experience, Mickey Cray had been asked to go into the swamps and capture as many of the intruder reptiles as he could. The state was paying decent money, but Mickey said no. He knew that every python he caught would be euthanized, and he couldn't bring himself to take part in that. He liked snakes too much. That was the problem.

He sat down on the ground near Beulah and she glided slowly in his direction. Her brick-sized head was elevated, the silky tongue flicking slowly.

Mickey grinned. "When's the last time you got fed?"

Beulah responded by clamping down on Mickey's left foot and throwing a meaty coil around both his legs.

"Easy, princess," he said.

The python wrapped upward with another coil, and then another. Mickey quickly locked both arms in front of his chest to protect his lungs from being crushed, but he was out of shape and Beulah was extremely powerful.

"Wahoo!" he hollered. "Yo!"

"What?" called a voice from the house.

"Get your butt out here!"

The snake was chewing on Mickey's foot as if it were a rabbit. He knew better than to struggle, for that would only cause Beulah to tighten her grip.

Wahoo came running. When he saw what the python was doing to his father, he yelled, "Don't move!"

"Oh, that's a good one," Mickey gasped. "I was thinking of dancing a jig."

"What the heck happened?"

"You forgot to feed her is what happened."

"No way! She ate last week, I swear, Pop."

"What did you give her—a cup of yogurt? Look at the poor girl, she's starving!"

Wahoo suspected his dad might be right—adult pythons often went weeks between meals. Maybe he *had* forgotten to feed her.

"Get the bleeping bourbon," Mickey said, "and make it fast." He was already gulping for air.

Wahoo ran back to the house and grabbed a bottle of liquor that his dad kept around for such emergencies. Pythons are equipped with rows of long, curved teeth that cannot be easily pried from their prey. The fastest way to make them let go is to pour something hot or obnoxious into their mouths.

Snakes don't have taste buds on their tongues like people do, so it wasn't the flavor of bourbon that Beulah hated. It was the sting. Wahoo got on his knees and sorted through the muscular coils until he located the toothy end of the creature, which had already swallowed half of his father's foot.

"You didn't even wear your boots?" Wahoo said.

Mickey grunted. "Get on with it already."

Wahoo uncapped the liquor bottle and dribbled the brown liquid directly down Beulah's throat. Within seconds the python began to twitch. Then she hissed loudly, unhooked her chompers and spit. Mickey purposely remained limp while Wahoo began unwinding the massive reptile.

Beulah didn't put up a struggle; she'd lost all interest in making a meal of Wahoo's father. The alcohol in the bourbon was highly irritating, and she kept opening and closing her mouth in distaste.

It took a few minutes for Mickey to catch his breath and for the circulation to return to his legs. He was able to hop along beside Wahoo as they lugged the big snake back to her tank. Then they went inside to take care of Mickey's foot, which looked like a purple pincushion.

"Promise you fed her? Tell the truth, son."

Wahoo felt awful. "I must have forgot."

"Springtime is when they get active and really start chowing down. I've only told you about a hundred times." With a groan, Mickey sprawled on the couch.

"Dad, I'm really sorry."

"Soon as we're done here, you go fetch her a couple of big fat chickens from the freezer. And nuke 'em good in the microwave, okay? Pythons don't like Popsicles."

"Yes, sir."

Wahoo emptied a tube of antiseptic ointment on his father's foot, and with a butter knife he spread the goop over all the puncture holes. There were too many to count. Pythons weren't poisonous, but a bite could cause a nasty infection.

"I'm sorry," Wahoo said again. "I really messed up."

"Enough already. Everybody makes mistakes," his dad told him. "Heck, I shouldn't have been playin' with a snake that size, like she was a fuzzy little poodle."

"Hold still, Pop."

Mickey stared up at the ceiling. "Look, I know this ain't exactly a normal life for a kid your age."

"Don't start again," Wahoo said.

"No, I mean it," Mickey went on. "What would I do without you and your mom? I'm lucky she stuck around all these years."

"Yes, you are. Where's the gauze?"

Wahoo waited until his dad's wounds were bandaged before telling him what Julie had said about the *Expedition Survival!* contract.

"I knew the guy was trouble," Mickey muttered.

"So what do we do now?"

"Our job, son. We do our job." Mickey levered himself up, swinging his puffy, snake-bitten foot up on the coffee table. "I don't care what their stupid paperwork says—I'm the only one in charge of my animals. Mr. Dork Badger can go fly a kite."

"It's *Derek* Badger."

"Ha! You think it matters to these critters what his stupid name is?"

"No, Pop."

"Know what Beulah would say? 'All you stupid humans taste the same!'"

Wahoo found himself wondering if that was really true.

QUESTIONS FOR CRITICAL THINKING AND WRITING

1. This excerpt includes five distinct characters: Derek Badger, Raven Stark, Wahoo Cray, Julie Cray, and Mickey Cray. How would you describe each character? Support your descriptions with specific references to the story.

2. Hiaasen uses humor throughout this excerpt, even when some of the circumstances are quite serious. Identify a place in the story where humor is used to great effect either during a difficult situation or after it unfolds. Why do you think the author chose to use the tone he did?

3. How is Derek Badger described? What do the details about his rise to stardom reveal about him — and the producers of *Expedition Survival!* — and how do they serve as a contrast to the Cray family?

CAROLINA HOSPITAL

For biographical information on Carolina Hospital, see page 1 of the Introduction.

BEFORE YOU READ

In "How the Cubans Stole Miami," Hospital's speaker uses somewhat derogatory terms to refer to minority groups. Why is this done, do you think? Are words or phrases like these appropriate in literature or other art? Where is the line between artistic and offensive drawn, in your opinion?

How the Cubans Stole Miami   *1994*

The Cubans have stolen Miami.
("Will the last one to leave
bring the American flag?")
And from whom did we steal it?

From the Basque sailor who   5
gave Biscayne its name?
Or perhaps from the Spanish missionaries who lived
with the mosquitoes by the swampy bay?

In all fairness, we must admit
we stole it from the Tequesta or the Seminoles,   10
natives, driven north by
Andrew Jackson or south into the sea.

No, perhaps we stole it from the Spaniards
sent back to Havana after 300 years
of calling Florida home.   15
(And we complain about still being
in exile after only thirty-four.)

If we didn't steal it from the Indians or the Spaniards
it must have been the Conks,
Bahamians who built the railroads with hands of coal   20
while being told to be more Negro like their
neighbors to the north.

I know, we stole it from
Flagler, Tuttle, Merrick and Fisher
who catered to the rich but never to the Jewish.   25
(Only in Miami is a Jew an Anglo.)
If I see one more photo of Domino Park
I'll turn into a Jew.

Was it he, papi, who stole Miami?
He, who engineered from the Bacardi building to   30
One Biscayne Tower
and every school addition from Edison
to Homestead High?

No, it must have been my mother.
(What was it Joan Didion wrote,   35
"a mango with jewels?"
poor mother, so lean and trim.)
She spent 34 years volunteering
(Sacándole el kilo, my father would sneer.)

The Museum of Science,   40
Viscaya,
The Youth Center,
The Archdiocese,
Ballet Concerto,
La Liga Contra el Cancer,   45
The Mailman Center.
(A tour of Miami, you ask?)

Enough! says my dad,
locking up his checkbook tight.
"We're retiring out of Miami."   50
A new phenomenon,
"Cuban Flight,"
not to be confused with "White Flight."

If the Cubans have stolen Miami
and it's time they paid their dues,   55
then . . .

If I see one more photograph of Domino Park
who knows what I might do.

QUESTIONS FOR CRITICAL THINKING AND WRITING

1. The narrator of the poem uses several rhetorical questions to ask from whom the Cubans stole Miami. What purpose do these rhetorical questions serve, and what do they lend to the tone of the poem?
2. "Domino Park" refers to a park in Little Havana, Miami. Why do you think the speaker is tired of seeing images of this park, and what do the images of this park represent to her?
3. What is meant by the phrase "Only in Miami is a Jew an Anglo"? What is the speaker saying about the ethnic makeup of the city?

ZORA NEALE HURSTON

Zora Neale Hurston (1891–1960) is considered one of the most prominent writers of twentieth-century American literature. Hurston was raised in Eatonville, Florida, and her Floridian background is featured heavily in her work. She is best known for her novel *Their Eyes Were Watching God* (1937), but she published more than fifty short stories, plays, and essays. Hurston was known almost as much for her engaging—and sometimes outrageous—personality; fellow author Sterling Brown said of Hurston, "When Zora was there, she was the party."

Courtesy of Library of Congress.

BEFORE YOU READ

Hurston's work was largely ignored for a period after her death, in part because of her use of black southern dialect and language. As you read this excerpt from her memoir, think about the difference between accurately representing the spoken word and furthering a stereotype or caricature through speech. Which does Hurston do here, in your opinion?

From *Mules and Men*   *1935*

As I crossed the Maitland-Eatonville township line I could see a group on the store porch. I was delighted. The town had not changed. Same love of talk and song. So I drove on down there before I stopped. Yes, there was George Thomas, Calvin Daniels, Jack and Charlie Jones, Gene Brazzle, B. Moseley and "Seaboard." Deep in a game of Florida-flip. All of those who were not actually playing were giving advice—"bet straightening" they call it.

"Hello, boys," I hailed them as I went into neutral.

They looked up from the game and for a moment it looked as if they had forgotten me. Then B. Moseley said, "Well, if it ain't Zora Hurston!" Then everybody crowded around the car to help greet me.

"You gointer stay awhile, Zora?"

"Yep. Several months."

"Where you gointer stay, Zora?"

"With Mett and Ellis, I reckon."

"Mett" was Mrs. Armetta Jones, an intimate friend of mine since childhood and Ellis was her husband. Their house stands under the huge camphor tree on the front street.

"Hello, heart-string," Mayor Hiram Lester yelled as he hurried up the street. "We heard all about you up North. You back home for good, I hope."

"Nope, Ah come to collect some old stories and tales and Ah know y'all know a plenty of 'em and that's why Ah headed straight for home."

"What you mean, Zora, them big old lies we tell when we're jus' sittin' around here on the store porch doin' nothin'?" asked B. Moseley.

"Yeah, those same ones about Ole Massa, and colored folks in heaven, and — oh, y'all know the kind I mean."

"Aw shucks," exclaimed George Thomas doubtfully. "Zora, don't you come here and tell de biggest lie first thing. Who you reckon want to read all them old-time tales about Brer Rabbit and Brer Bear?"

"Plenty of people, George. They are a lot more valuable than you might think. We want to set them down before it's too late."

"Too late for what?"

"Before everybody forgets all of 'em."

"No danger of that. That's all some people is good for — set 'round and lie and murder groceries."

"Ah know one right now," Calvin Daniels announced cheerfully. "It's a tale 'bout John and de frog."

"Wait till she get out her car, Calvin. Let her get settled at 'Met's' and cook a pan of ginger bread then we'll all go down and tell lies and eat ginger bread. Dat's de way to do. She's tired now from all dat drivin'."

"All right, boys," I agreed. "But Ah'll be rested by night. Be lookin' for everybody."

So I unloaded the car and crowded it into Ellis' garage and got settled. Armetta made me lie down and rest while she cooked a big pan of ginger bread for the company we expected.

Questions for Critical Thinking and Writing

1. B. Moseley calls the stories Hurston wants to record "big old lies." Why does Hurston believe these "lies" to be important, and why does she want to record them?

2. How does Hurston set the scene in the first paragraph? What might a reader expect from a scene like this?

3. Hurston states that upon returning, she was glad to see that the town had the "same love of talk and song." In your opinion, has this "love," or the expression of it, changed since Hurston was writing? Is it still as culturally relevant as it once was?

Zora Neale Hurston

A biographical note for Zora Neale Hurston appears on page 79.

Before You Read

As you read, keep in mind that "Sweat" can be considered a folktale. It shares many features with more traditional folktales, including specific community values, local dialect, and a moral lesson at the end. Think about where "Sweat" is similar to a folktale, and where it differs.

Sweat

I

It was eleven o'clock of a Spring night in Florida. It was Sunday. Any other night, Delia Jones would have been in bed for two hours by this time. But she was a washwoman, and Monday morning meant a great deal to her. So she collected the soiled clothes on Saturday when she returned the clean things. Sunday night after church, she sorted and put the white things to soak. It saved her almost a half-day's start. A great hamper in the bedroom held the clothes that she brought home. It was so much neater than a number of bundles lying around.

She squatted on the kitchen floor beside the great pile of clothes, sorting them into small heaps according to color, and humming a song in a mournful key, but wondering through it all where Sykes, her husband, had gone with her horse and buckboard.

Just then something long, round, limp, and black fell upon her shoulders and slithered to the floor beside her. A great terror took hold of her. It softened her knees and dried her mouth so that it was a full minute before she could cry out or move. Then she saw that it was the big bull whip her husband liked to carry when he drove.

She lifted her eyes to the door and saw him standing there bent over with laughter at her fright. She screamed at him.

"Sykes, what you throw dat whip on me like dat? You know it would skeer me—looks just like a snake, an' you knows how skeered Ah is of snakes."

"Course Ah knowed it! That's how come Ah done it." He slapped his leg with his hand and almost rolled on the ground in his mirth. "If you such a big fool dat you got to have a fit over a earth worm or a string, Ah don't keer how bad Ah skeer you."

"You ain't got no business doing it. Gawd knows it's a sin. Some day Ah'm gointuh drop dead from some of yo' foolishness. 'Nother thing, where you been wid mah rig? Ah feeds dat pony. He ain't fuh you to be drivin' wid no bull whip."

"You sho' is one aggravatin' nigger woman!" he declared and stepped into the room. She resumed her work and did not answer him at once. "Ah done tole you time and again to keep them white folks' clothes outa dis house."

He picked up the whip and glared at her. Delia went on with her work. She went out into the yard and returned with a galvanized tub and set it on the washbench. She saw that Sykes had kicked all of the clothes together again, and now stood in her way truculently, his whole manner hoping, *praying*, for an argument. But she walked calmly around him and commenced to re-sort the things.

"Next time, Ah'm gointer kick 'em outdoors," he threatened as he struck a match along the leg of his corduroy breeches.

Delia never looked up from her work, and her thin, stooped shoulders sagged further.

"Ah ain't for no fuss t'night, Sykes. Ah just come from taking sacrament at the church house."

He snorted scornfully. "Yeah, you just come from de church house on a Sunday night, but heah you is gone to work on them clothes. You ain't nothing but a hypocrite. One of them amen-corner Christians—sing, whoop, and shout, then come home and wash white folks' clothes on the Sabbath."

He stepped roughly upon the whitest pile of things, kicking them helter-skelter as he crossed the room. His wife gave a little scream of dismay, and quickly gathered them together again.

"Sykes, you quit grindin' dirt into these clothes! How can Ah git through by Sat'day if Ah don't start on Sunday?"

"Ah don't keer if you never git through. Anyhow, Ah done promised Gawd and a couple of other men, Ah ain't gointer have it in mah house. Don't gimme no lip neither, else Ah'll throw 'em out and put mah fist up side yo' head to boot."

Delia's habitual meekness seemed to slip from her shoulders like a blown scarf. She was on her feet; her poor little body, her bare knuckly hands bravely defying the strapping hulk before her.

"Looka heah, Sykes, you done gone too fur. Ah been married to you fur fifteen years, and Ah been takin' in washin' fur fifteen years. Sweat, sweat, sweat! Work and sweat, cry and sweat, pray and sweat!"

"What's that got to do with me?" he asked brutally.

"What's it got to do with you, Sykes? Mah tub of suds is filled yo' belly with vittles more times than yo' hands is filled it. Mah sweat is done paid for this house and Ah reckon Ah kin keep on sweatin' in it."

She seized the iron skillet from the stove and struck a defensive pose, which act surprised him greatly, coming from her. It cowed him and he did not strike her as he usually did.

"Naw you won't," she panted, "that ole snaggle-toothed black woman you runnin' with ain't comin' heah to pile up on *mah* sweat and blood. You ain't paid for nothin' on this place, and Ah'm gointer stay right heah till Ah'm toted out foot foremost."

"Well, you better quit gittin' me riled up, else they'll be totin' you out sooner than you expect. Ah'm so tired of you Ah don't know whut to do. Gawd! How Ah hates skinny wimmen!"

A little awed by this new Delia, he sidled out of the door and slammed the back gate after him. He did not say where he had gone, but she knew too well. She knew very well that he would not return until nearly daybreak also. Her work over, she went on to bed but not to sleep at once. Things had come to a pretty pass!

She lay awake, gazing upon the debris that cluttered their matrimonial trail. Not an image left standing along the way. Anything like flowers had long ago been drowned in the salty stream that had been pressed from her heart. Her tears, her sweat, her blood. She had brought love to the union and he had brought a longing after the flesh. Two months after the wedding, he had given her the first brutal beating. She had the memory of his numerous trips to Orlando with all of his wages when he had returned to her penniless, even before the first year had passed. She was young and soft then, but now she thought of her knotty, muscled limbs, her harsh knuckly hands, and drew herself up into an unhappy little ball in the middle of the big feather bed. Too late now to hope for love, even if it were not Bertha it would be someone else. This case differed from the others only in that she was bolder than the others. Too late for everything except her little home. She had built it for her old days, and planted one by one the trees and flowers there. It was lovely to her, lovely.

Somehow, before sleep came, she found herself saying aloud: "Oh well, whatever goes over the Devil's back, is got to come under his belly. Sometime or ruther, Sykes, like everybody else, is gointer reap his sowing." After that she was able to build a spiritual earthworks against her husband. His shells could no longer reach her. Amen. She went to sleep and slept until he announced his presence in bed by kicking her feet and rudely snatching the covers away.

"Gimme some kivah heah, an' git yo' damn foots over on yo' own side! Ah oughter mash you in yo' mouf fuh drawing dat skillet on me."

Delia went clear to the rail without answering him. A triumphant indifference to all that he was or did.

II

The week was full of work for Delia as all other weeks, and Saturday found her behind her little pony, collecting and delivering clothes.

It was a hot, hot day near the end of July. The village men on Joe Clarke's porch even chewed cane listlessly. They did not hurl the cane-knots as usual. They let them dribble over the edge of the porch. Even conversation had collapsed under the heat.

"Heah come Delia Jones," Jim Merchant said, as the shaggy pony came 'round the bend of the road toward them. The rusty buckboard was heaped with baskets of crisp, clean laundry.

"Yep," Joe Lindsay agreed. "Hot or col', rain or shine, jes'ez reg'lar ez de weeks roll roun' Delia carries 'em an' fetches 'em on Sat'day."

"She better if she wanter eat," said Moss. "Syke Jones ain't wuth de shot an' powder hit would tek tuh kill 'em. Not to *huh* he ain't."

"He sho' ain't," Walter Thomas chimed in. "It's too bad, too, cause she wuz a right pretty li'l trick when he got huh. Ah'd uh mah'ied huh mahself if he hadnter beat me to it."

Delia nodded briefly at the men as she drove past.

"Too much knockin' will ruin *any* 'oman. He done beat huh 'nough tuh kill three women, let 'lone change they looks," said Elijah Moseley. "How Syke kin stommuck dat big black greasy Mogul he's layin' roun' wid, gits me. Ah swear dat eight-rock couldn't kiss a sardine can Ah done thowed out de back do' 'way las' yeah."

"Aw, she's fat, thass how come. He's allus been crazy 'bout fat women," put in Merchant. "He'd a' been tied up wid one long time ago if he could a' found one tuh have him. Did Ah tell yuh 'bout him come sidlin' roun' *mah* wife—bringin' her a basket uh peecans outa his yard fuh a present? Yessir, mah wife! She tol' him tuh take 'em right straight back home, 'cause Delia works so hard ovah dat washtub she reckon everything on de place taste lak sweat an' soapsuds. Ah jus' wisht Ah'd a' caught 'im roun' dere! Ah'd a' made his hips ketch on fiah down dat shell road."

"Ah know he done it, too. Ah sees 'im grinnin' at every 'oman dat passes," Walter Thomas said. "But even so, he useter eat some mighty big hunks uh humble pie tuh git dat li'l 'oman he got. She wuz ez pritty ez a speckled pup! Dat wuz fifteen years ago. He useter be so skeered uh losin' huh, she could make him do some parts of a husband's duty. Dey never wuz de same in de mind."

"There oughter be a law about him," said Lindsay. "He ain't fit tuh carry guts tuh a bear."

Clarke spoke for the first time. "Tain't no law on earth dat kin make a man be decent if it ain't in 'im. There's plenty men dat takes a wife lak dey do a joint uh sugar-cane. It's round, juicy, an' sweet when dey gits it. But dey squeeze an' grind, squeeze an' grind an' wring tell dey wring every drop uh pleasure dat's in 'em out. When dey's satisfied dat dey is wrung dry, dey treats 'em jes' lak dey do a cane-chew. Dey thows 'em away. Dey knows whut dey is doin' while dey is at it, an' hates theirselves fuh it but they keeps on hangin' after huh tell she's empty. Den dey hates huh fuh bein' a cane-chew an' in de way."

"We oughter take Syke an' dat stray 'oman uh his'n down in Lake Howell swamp an' lay on de rawhide till they cain't say Lawd a' mussy. He allus wuz uh ovahbearin niggah, but since dat white 'oman from up north done teached 'im how to run a automobile, he done got too beggety to live—an' we oughter kill 'im," Old Man Anderson advised.

A grunt of approval went around the porch. But the heat was melting their civic virtue and Elijah Moseley began to bait Joe Clarke.

"Come on, Joe, git a melon outa dere an' slice it up for yo' customers. We'se all sufferin' wid de heat. De bear's done got *me!*"

"Thass right, Joe, a watermelon is jes' whut Ah needs tuh cure de eppizudicks," Walter Thomas joined forces with Moseley. "Come on dere, Joe. We all is steady customers an' you ain't set us up in a long time. Ah chooses dat long, bowlegged Floridy favorite."

"A god, an' be dough. You all gimme twenty cents and slice away," Clarke retorted. "Ah needs a col' slice m'self. Heah, everybody chip in. Ah'll lend y'all mah meat knife."

The money was all quickly subscribed and the huge melon brought forth. At that moment, Sykes and Bertha arrived. A determined silence fell on the porch and the melon was put away again.

Merchant snapped down the blade of his jacknife and moved toward the store door.

"Come on in, Joe, an' gimme a slab uh sow belly an' uh pound uh coffee— almost fuhgot 'twas Sat'day. Got to git on home." Most of the men left also.

Just then Delia drove past on her way home, as Sykes was ordering magnificently for Bertha. It pleased him for Delia to see.

"Git whutsoever yo' heart desires, Honey. Wait a minute, Joe. Give huh two bottles uh strawberry soda-water, uh quart parched ground-peas, an' a block uh chewin' gum."

With all this they left the store, with Sykes reminding Bertha that this was his town and she could have it if she wanted it.

The men returned soon after they left, and held their watermelon feast.

"Where did Syke Jones git da 'oman from nohow?" Lindsay asked.

"Ovah Apopka. Guess dey musta been cleanin' out de town when she lef'. She don't look lak a thing but a hunk uh liver wid hair on it."

"Well, she sho' kin squall," Dave Carter contributed. "When she gits ready tuh laff, she jes' opens huh mouf an' latches it back tuh de las' notch. No ole granpa alligator down in Lake Bell ain't got nothin' on huh."

III

Bertha had been in town three months now. Sykes was still paying her room-rent at Della Lewis'—the only house in town that would have taken her in. Sykes took her frequently to Winter Park to "stomps." He still assured her that he was the swellest man in the state.

"Sho' you kin have dat li'l ole house soon's Ah git dat 'oman outa dere. Everything b'longs tuh me an' you sho' kin have it. Ah sho' 'bominates uh skinny 'oman. Lawdy, you sho' is got one portly shape on you! You kin git *anything* you wants. Dis is *mah* town an' you sho' kin have it."

Delia's work-worn knees crawled over the earth in Gethsemane[1] and up the rocks of Calvary many, many times during these months. She avoided the villagers and meeting places in her efforts to be blind and deaf. But Bertha nullified this to a degree, by coming to Delia's house to call Sykes out to her at the gate.

Delia and Sykes fought all the time now with no peaceful interludes. They slept and ate in silence. Two or three times Delia had attempted a timid friendliness, but she was repulsed each time. It was plain that the breaches must remain agape.

---

[1] Gethsemane is the garden where, according to the Bible, Jesus and his disciples prayed the night before Jesus was crucified on Calvary (which is also known as Golgotha, "the place of the skull").

The sun had burned July to August. The heat streamed down like a million hot arrows, smiting all things living upon the earth. Grass withered, leaves browned, snakes went blind in shedding, and men and dogs went mad. Dog days!

Delia came home one day and found Sykes there before her. She wondered, but started to go on into the house without speaking, even though he was standing in the kitchen door and she must either stoop under his arm or ask him to move. He made no room for her. She noticed a soap box beside the steps, but paid no particular attention to it, knowing that he must have brought it there. As she was stooping to pass under his outstretched arm, he suddenly pushed her backward, laughingly.

"Look in de box dere Delia, Ah done brung yuh somethin'!"

She nearly fell upon the box in her stumbling, and when she saw what it held, she all but fainted outright.

"Syke! Syke, mah Gawd! You take dat rattlesnake 'way from heah! You *gottuh*. Oh, Jesus, have mussy!"

"Ah ain't got tuh do nuthin' uh de kin'—fact is Ah ain't got tuh do nothin' but die. Tain't no use uh you puttin' on airs makin' out lak you skeered uh dat snake—he's gointer stay right heah tell he die. He wouldn't bite me cause Ah knows how tuh handle 'im. Nohow he wouldn't risk breakin' out his fangs 'gin *yo* skinny laigs."

"Naw, now Syke, don't keep dat thing 'round tryin' tuh skeer me tuh death. You knows Ah'm even feared uh earth worms. Thass de biggest snake Ah evah did se. Kill 'im Syke, please."

"Doan ast me tuh do nothin' fuh yuh. Goin' 'round tryin' tuh be so damn asterperious. Naw, Ah ain't gonna kill it. Ah think uh damn sight mo' uh him dan you! Dat's a nice snake an' anybody doan lak 'im kin jes' hit de grit."

The village soon heard that Sykes had the snake, and came to see and ask questions.

"How de hen-fire did you ketch dat six-foot rattler, Syke?" Thomas asked.

"He's full uh frogs so he cain't hardly move, thass how Ah eased up on 'im. But Ah'm a snake charmer an' knows how tuh handle 'em. Shux, dat ain't nothin'. Ah could ketch one eve'y day if Ah so wanted tuh."

"Whut he needs is a heavy hick'ry club leaned real heavy on his head. Dat's de bes' way tuh charm a rattlesnake."

"Naw, Walt, y'all jes' don't understand dese diamon' backs lak Ah do," said Sykes in a superior tone of voice.

The village agreed with Walter, but the snake stayed on. His box remained by the kitchen door with its screen wire covering. Two or three days later it had digested its meal of frogs and literally came to life. It rattled at every movement in the kitchen or the yard. One day as Delia came down the kitchen steps she saw his chalky-white fangs curved like scimitars hung in the wire meshes. This time she did not run away with averted eyes as usual. She stood for a long time in the doorway in a red fury that grew bloodier for every second that she regarded the creature that was her torment.

That night she broached the subject as soon as Sykes sat down to the table.

"Syke, Ah wants you tuh take dat snake 'way fum heah. You done starved me an' Ah put up widcher, you done beat me an Ah took dat, but you don kilt all mah insides bringin' dat varmint heah."

Sykes poured out a saucer full of coffee and drank it deliberately before he answered her.

"A whole lot Ah keer 'bout how you feels inside uh out. Dat snake ain't goin' no damn wheah till Ah gits ready fuh 'im tuh go. So fur as beatin' is concerned, yuh ain't took near all dat you gointer take ef yuh stay 'round *me*."

Delia pushed back her plate and got up from the table. "Ah hates you, Sykes," she said calmly. "Ah hates you tuh de same degree dat Ah useter love yuh. Ah done took an' took till mah belly is full up tuh mah neck. Dat's de reason Ah got mah letter fum de church an' moved mah membership tuh Woodbridge—so Ah don't haftuh take no sacrament wid yuh. Ah don't wantuh see yuh 'round me atall. Lay 'round wid dat 'oman all yuh wants tuh, but gwan 'way from me an' mah house. Ah hates yuh lak uh suck-egg dog."

Sykes almost let the huge wad of corn bread and collard greens he was chewing fall out of his mouth in amazement. He had a hard time whipping himself up to the proper fury to try to answer Delia.

"Well, Ah'm glad you does hate me. Ah'm sho' tiahed uh you hangin' ontuh me. Ah don't want yuh. Look at yuh stringey ole neck! Yo' rawbony laigs an' arms is enough tuh cut uh man tuh death. You looks jes' lak de devvul's doll-baby tuh *me*. You cain't hate me no worse dan Ah hates you. Ah been hatin' *you* fuh years."

"Yo' ole black hide don't look lak nothin' tuh me, but uh passle uh wrinkled up rubber, wid yo' big ole yeahs flappin' on each side lak uh paih uh buzzard wings. Don't think Ah'm gointuh be run 'way fum mah house neither. Ah'm goin' tuh de white folks 'bout *you*, mah young man, de very nex' time you lay yo' han's on me. Mah cup is done run ovah." Delia said this with no signs of fear and Sykes departed from the house, threatening her, but made not the slightest move to carry out any of them.

That night he did not return at all, and the next day being Sunday, Delia was glad she did not have to quarrel before she hitched up her pony and drove the four miles to Woodbridge.

She stayed to the night service—"love feast"—which was very warm and full of spirit. In the emotional winds her domestic trials were borne far and wide so that she sang as she drove homeward,

Jurden water, black an' col
Chills de body, not de soul
An'Ah wantah cross Jurden in uh calm time.

She came from the barn to the kitchen door and stopped.

"Whut's de mattah, ol' Satan, you ain't kicken' up yo' racket?" She addressed the snake's box. Complete silence. She went on into the house with a new hope in its birth struggles. Perhaps her threat to go to the white folks had frightened Sykes! Perhaps he was sorry! Fifteen years of misery and suppression had brought Delia to the place where she would hope *anything* that looked towards a way over or through her wall of inhibitions.

She felt in the match-safe behind the stove at once for a match. There was only one there.

"Dat niggah wouldn't fetch nothin' heah tuh save his rotten neck, but he kin run thew whut Ah brings quick enough. Now he done toted off nigh on tuh haff uh box uh matches. He done had dat 'oman heah in mah house, too."

Nobody but a woman could tell how she knew this even before she struck the match. But she did and it put her into a new fury.

Presently she brought in the tubs to put the white things to soak. This time she decided she need not bring the hamper out of the bedroom; she would go in there and do the sorting. She picked up the pot-bellied lamp and went in. The room was small and the hamper stood hard by the foot of the white iron bed. She could sit and reach through the bedposts—resting as she worked.

"Ah wantah cross Jurden in uh calm time." She was singing again. The mood of the "love feast" had returned. She threw back the lid of the basket almost gaily.

Then, moved by both horror and terror, she sprang back toward the door. *There lay the snake in the basket!* He moved sluggishly at first, but even as she turned round and round, jumped up and down in an insanity of fear, he began to stir vigorously. She saw him pouring his awful beauty from the basket upon the bed, then she seized the lamp and ran as fast as she could to the kitchen. The wind from the open door blew out the light and the darkness added to her terror. She sped to the darkness of the yard, slamming the door after her before she thought to set down the lamp. She did not feel safe even on the ground, so she climbed up in the hay barn.

There for an hour or more she lay sprawled upon the hay a gibbering wreck.

Finally she grew quiet, and after that came coherent thought. With this stalked through her a cold, bloody rage. Hours of this. A period of introspection, a space of retrospection, then a mixture of both. Out of this an awful calm.

"Well, Ah done de bes' Ah could. If things ain't right, Gawd knows tain't mah fault."

She went to sleep—a twitch sleep—and woke up to a faint gray sky. There was a loud hollow sound below. She peered out. Sykes was at the woodpile, demolishing a wire-covered box.

He hurried to the kitchen door, but hung outside there some minutes before he entered, and stood some minutes more inside before he closed it after him.

The gray in the sky was spreading. Delia descended without fear now, and crouched beneath the low bedroom window. The drawn shade shut out the dawn, shut in the night. But the thin walls held back no sound.

"Dat ol' scratch is woke up now!" She mused at the tremendous whirr inside, which every woodsman knows, is one of the sound illusions. The rattler is a ventriloquist. His whirr sounds to the right, to the left, straight ahead, behind, close under foot—everywhere but where it is. Woe to him who guesses wrong unless he is prepared to hold up his end of the argument! Sometimes he strikes without rattling at all.

Inside, Sykes heard nothing until he knocked a pot lid off the stove while trying to reach the match-safe in the dark. He had emptied his pockets at Bertha's.

The snake seemed to wake up under the stove and Sykes made a quick leap into the bedroom. In spite of the gin he had had, his head was clearing now.

"Mah Gawd!" he chattered, "ef Ah could on'y strack uh light!"

The rattling ceased for a moment as he stood paralyzed. He waited. It seemed that the snake waited also.

"Oh, fuh de light! Ah thought he'd be too sick"—Sykes was muttering to himself when the whirr began again, closer, right underfoot this time. Long before this, Sykes' ability to think had been flattened down to primitive instinct and he leaped—onto the bed.

Outside Delia heard a cry that might have come from a maddened chimpanzee, a stricken gorilla. All the terror, all the horror, all the rage that man possibly could express, without a recognizable human sound.

A tremendous stir inside there, another series of animal screams, the intermittent whirr of the reptile. The shade torn violently down from the window, letting in the red dawn, a huge brown hand seizing the window stick, great dull blows upon the wooden floor punctuating the gibberish of sound long after the rattle of the snake had abruptly subsided. All this Delia could see and hear from her place beneath the window, and it made her ill. She crept over to the four o'clocks and stretched herself on the cool earth to recover.

She lay there. "Delia, Delia!" She could hear Sykes calling in a most despairing tone as one who expected no answer. The sun crept on up, and he called.

Delia could not move — her legs had gone flabby. She never moved, he called, and the sun kept rising.

"Mah Gawd!" She heard him moan, "Mah Gawd fum Heben!" She heard him stumbling about and got up from her flower-bed. The sun was growing warm. As she approached the door she heard him call out hopefully, "Delia, is dat you Ah heah?"

She saw him on his hands and knees as soon as she reached the door. He crept an inch or two toward her — all that he was able, and she saw his horribly swollen neck and his one open eye shining with hope. A surge of pity too strong to support bore her away from that eye that must, could not, fail to see the tubs. He would see the lamp. Orlando with its doctors was too far. She could scarcely reach the chinaberry tree, where she waited in the growing heat while inside she knew the cold river was creeping up and up to extinguish that eye which must know by now that she knew.

QUESTIONS FOR CRITICAL THINKING AND WRITING

1. What purpose does the chorus of men on the porch serve? Why does Hurston include their thoughts and judgments about Delia and Sykes's marriage?

2. How does Delia's fear of snakes relate to other aspects of her character? Why does Hurston give her that specific fear, and how is it symbolic?

3. What is the significance of Delia's status as a washwoman? Why is her occupation important to the action of the story, and how does it help the reader to understand the rift between Delia and Sykes?

GLORIA JAHODA

Gloria Jahoda (1926–1980) was a Floridian author and historian. Her history of the Hillsborough River, *River of the Golden Ibis*, was recognized as the best history book of the year by the Society of Midland Authors of Florida in 1973. Jahoda is also known for exposing the history of lesser-known parts of Florida, especially the north-central region. In 1973, Jahoda was awarded an honorary doctorate by the University of West Florida for her contributions to Floridian history.

Courtesy of the State Archives of Florida.

BEFORE YOU READ

In the following essay, Gloria Jahoda relates one man's argument that the original Garden of Eden was located in what is now Bristol, Florida. What are the implications of trying to prove the physical location of a place in the Old Testament, and why might someone work so hard and devote so much of his life to proving this argument?

From *The Garden of Eden* 1967

It is about 50 miles northeast of Panama City, near Bristol, that the quality of the landscape changes, and the change is startling. Suddenly you are driving through tracts of timberland where the pines are old and immense. The ground begins gently to rise in little hills that swell to steep bluffs along the Apalachicola river, and hickories and swamp maples tower over a carpet of leafmold which only the feet of hunters and botanists and moonshine makers have disturbed. Large patches of this forest are virgin. Here too are mixed the palms of the tropics and the hardwoods of the Appalachian mountains to the north, the lacy ferns of a prehistoric torrid zone and the familiar arbutuses and lobelias of temperate woods, and a few enigmas of the plant world which can be found nowhere else on earth.

"It was right here in Bristol, Florida," Elvy E. Callaway told me one afternoon as we sat on his porch. Beyond us, tall laurel oaks were thickly festooned with bunches of lavender wisteria, and birdsfoot violets were blooming at the edge of the woods. "The original Garden of Eden was here on the banks of the Apalachicola. God created the Adamic man one mile east of Bristol and breathed into his nostrils the breath of life and then gave him a soul. Then He created the Garden of Eden just north of town and as the Bible says, 'out of the ground He caused to grow every tree pleasant to the sight'—including the gopher wood trees. There's only one place in the world they grow. That's here in Bristol. Some people call them Torrey trees."

Mr. Callaway, for many years a lawyer for the NAACP and an ordained Baptist minister, is a native Southerner. His great-uncle was Confederate General John Bell Hood. He is not a conformist. In 1936 he ran for Florida's governorship on the Republican ticket. He shared the fate of presidential aspirant Alf M. Landon in that year of a one-party South, but he believes fate had more important plans for him than politics.

"I was chosen and directed to uncover the evidence in absolute proof of the Bible account of purposeful creation." It was also in Bristol, Florida, that Noah built his ark. "It was built of gopher wood as the Bible says, and pitched with its pitch. After the earth was covered with water in the flood it floated for five months to Mount Ararat in Asia where it landed. That's when Noah gave Asia the place names he'd known in Florida, like Euphrates."

And how, I asked Mr. Callaway, had he arrived at these startling conclusions, which I had found to be shared by an impressive number of north Floridians?

"I've spent seventy-five years studying the question," he assured me. "People come to me doubting but they go away believing. First, the Bible tells us that 'a river went out of Eden to water the Garden and parted and became four heads.' It's all in Genesis 2. Well, the Apalachicola is the only four-head river system in the world. The U.S. Army Engineers' map shows you that. Second, the Bible says there were onyx and bdellium, or pitch, and good gold in the land. Now, the best gold in the world is found in north Georgia, where the Chattahoochee has its source before it flows into the Apalachicola. I've panned that gold myself. There's marble up there too. Four rivers—the Chattahoochee, the Fish Pond Creek, the Spring Creek, and the Flint—they all flow into the Apalachicola on the Georgia-Florida border, in Liberty and Jackson counties. You can see it at the Jim Woodruff dam."

To clinch his argument, he showed me a testimonial by the late A. R. Jones, Ph.D., of Eclectic, Alabama, author of *Man Before the Flood*, who died at 98 in 1964. "The Garden's location along the east bank of the Apalachicola river between Bristol and Chattahoochee, Florida, is now definite," says Dr. Jones. "These facts NAIL DOWN BEYOND INTELLIGENT CONTRADICTION [the capitals are his] that this is the exact location of the Original Garden of Eden, and the birthplace of our first parents, and the place where Noah made the Ark of gopher wood." Maybe, said Mr. Callaway, I'd already heard of gopher wood, or the Torrey tree.

I had, as I'd heard too that Mr. Callaway had offered Senator Barry Goldwater a retirement farm near the Garden of Eden on a certain Wednesday in November, 1964. 1936 was gone but not forgotten. If Senator Goldwater had ever seen the Garden of Eden, he might have considered accepting. In its vicinity of misty coves and flower-covered forest paths there is the strangeness and enchantment of a botanical never-never land. The *Torreya taxifolia* (*taxifolia* means yew-leaved) which grows there is one of the rarest trees in existence. And whether or not you can accept the idea that Adam and Eve hailed from Liberty county or that Noah made his Ark of Torreya wood, there is enough wonder in the tree itself and enough attraction in the place to make it a nature-lover's Garden of Eden.

QUESTIONS FOR CRITICAL THINKING AND WRITING

1. Much of this essay is directly quoted from the sources. Why might Jahoda have presented so much dialogue and so little analysis in this situation? How does hearing the argument directly from the believer affect your reading?

2. Because Elvy Callaway's views are presented in his own words, the reader is very aware of his strong belief in the idea that the original Garden of Eden was located in Bristol. How does Callaway come across in this essay? Is he reasonable? Scientific? Eccentric? What, specifically, makes you come to these conclusions about his character?

3. Jahoda does not explicitly state whether she believes Callaway's argument. Do you get a sense of whether she finds his argument valid, or does she maintain a neutral stance throughout? How so?

GLORIA JAHODA

A biographical note for Gloria Jahoda appears on page 88.

BEFORE YOU READ

Gloria Jahoda writes in a style that readers don't typically see in "history books." As you read this essay, make note of the ways in which Jahoda engages the reader through language, rather than simply relating facts.

From *Marshes and Moonports* 1976

People who do not believe in the adaptability of many species of wildlife gape when they visit the modern Merritt Island National Wildlife Refuge, which comprises 145,000 acres of land. Its bird and animal tenants — migratory waterfowl, raccoons and bobcats and alligators and feral pigs — have accepted rocket blast-offs with ease. (At Countdown Zero, the 'gators bellow handsomely.) Shore birds and ducks build their nests within sight of launch pads. There are even such endangered species as the bald eagle, the dusky seaside sparrow, and the peregrine falcon circling overhead. More than 195 birds were identified on one Christmas count by the Indian River Audubon Society. The alligators in the pool in front of NASA headquarters have become addicted to marshmallows, the remains of peanut-butter sandwiches, and bologna; NASA employees feed them assiduously, though not always with what an alligator ought to be eating.

The beginnings of the Space Center were slow, but Russia speeded things up when she launched Sputnik I on October 4, 1957. America was electrified. The Communists had a technology of rocketry far ahead of anything the United States had produced. Communists on the moon! Panic set in rapidly in America. It was accelerated when Sputnik II went up with a dog inside it on November 3, 1957. American comics produced a reigning joke: What is the difference between Sputnik and a hamburger? With Sputnik, you *know* there's a dog inside. Russia had participated in the International Geophysical Year with a vengeance, and the race for space was on. Congress wanted to know how the United States had fallen behind. Educators, industrialists, and newspapers demanded action. Schools of Engineering sprang up in American universities at an unprecedented rate. In the spring of 1958, the United States launched a forlorn little eight-pound Vanguard satellite which, like its predecessor the Explorer, was a feeble echo of the Russian achievement. American booster rockets didn't have the thrust Russian rockets had. Russia followed Sputnik with the *Luna* series; Luna II impacted the moon in the autumn of 1959. On April 12, 1961, Yuri Gagarin, the first cosmonaut, was launched in Vostok I. By this time, John F. Kennedy had succeeded Dwight Eisenhower as president, and Kennedy was a man of action. America must begin launching heavy space vehicles immediately. Kennedy summoned three men who, between them, had spent three quarters of a century in rocketry: Dr. Kurt H. Debus, Theodor A. Poppel, and Georg von Tiesenhausen. Later, others were added to the planning and counseling group; Albert Zeiler and Wernher von Braun were among them. "That good old American know-how has gone to work," satirist Tom Lehrer observed about the German scientists who were veterans of Hitler's Peenemund rocket station.

NASA had come into existence, and the Kennedy Space Center on Cape Canaveral started expanding at a breath-taking rate. Overnight, Cocoa Beach and Titusville became cities full of technological wizards and their neglected wives — Space Center widows who tried everything from playing bridge to drinking southern bourbon to soothe their loneliness. So scientific was the atmosphere that, when the inevitable call girls arrived, they set up a complex co-ordinate index of each lady's talents and preferences. Traffic in Cocoa Beach and Titusville was a maze, and once-quiet roads witnessed the construction of Satellite Motels with Universe bars. Project Apollo, the manned lunar expedition, was devouring men and materials even as it was bringing chaos into what had been the dreaming Indian and Banana River country. Now the bananas rustled their flopping leaves not only on riverbanks, but on patios where the conversation centered on miniaturizing, the thermal stability of fuels, and Who Was Who back in Germany, from which 120 of the top scientists had come. And the Germans charmed Florida; they were soft-spoken and polite, their work was the romance of the age, and everybody in the area of Brevard County and Cape Canaveral was prospering mightily. Professor Charles Fairbanks of the University of Florida noted that, near Canaveral, Western civilization had come to the new world — from the east, since western Indians were not supposed to have had much civilization, particularly not the Ais. Now that same Western civilization would go out from Canaveral to other worlds.

Today, the Kennedy Space Center is staggering. It is also terrifying, with its intricate towers and immense ocean vessels, called Guppies, which transport spacecraft components, its columns of white fire and its earthshaking roars when rockets are launched, its mazes of buildings and laboratories and simulated moons. By September 1968, NASA employed 26,000 administrators, engineers and technicians and also a Civil Service planning and co-ordinating group numbering thousands. Eight hundred million dollars of government money had made Cape Canaveral into the staggering miracle that nonpluses, terrifies, intrigues, and finally defeats, for the sensitive, all human attempts to measure it or what its possibilities mean. Life in other solar systems? Undiscovered intelligent races? The total destruction of humankind? Perhaps the people most comfortable with the spectacle are nonintellectual tourists fresh from Florida Mermaid shows who are placid enough, in their air-conditioned buses, to wonder mostly about the possibility of Little Green Men.

QUESTIONS FOR CRITICAL THINKING AND WRITING

1. Many of the ideas in this essay are somewhat dated and reflect the time period in which it was published. Name a few, and explain why it might be important to read historical texts — specifically this essay — in the context of a different cultural atmosphere.

2. Why might Jahoda have included the detail about the NASA employees feeding alligators? What point is she illustrating here?

3. What, according to Jahoda, has Cape Canaveral come to represent?

4. **CONNECT TO ANOTHER READING.** How do Gloria Jahoda's descriptions and implied beliefs about the natural world interacting with the world we have created compare to those of Anne E. Rowe (p. 59)? How does Rowe's comment on the natural versus the imaginative apply to Jahoda's essay?

JAMES WELDON JOHNSON

James Weldon Johnson (1871–1938) was born in Jacksonville, Florida. Although Johnson was African American at a time when inequality was pervasive, he had the opportunity to study literature and music at Atlanta University. After graduation, he became the principal of a high school in Jacksonville and began his writing career on the side. *The Autobiography of an Ex-Colored Man* was published in 1912 (although originally under a pseudonym). Johnson was also a civil rights activist and took the position of national organizer for the NAACP in 1920.

Courtesy of Charles H. Phillips/Time & Life Pictures/Getty Images.

BEFORE YOU READ

The Autobiography of an Ex-Colored Man is actually a novel that tells the story of a man who sacrifices his identity for material wealth and success in the white community. How might this excerpt prepare the reader for what is to come?

From *The Autobiography of an Ex-Colored Man*   *1912*

At one of the first public balls I attended I saw the Pullman car porter who had so kindly assisted me in getting to Jacksonville. I went immediately to one of my factory friends and borrowed fifteen dollars with which to repay the loan my benefactor had made me. After I had given him the money, and was thanking him, I noticed that he wore what was, at least, an exact duplicate of my lamented black and gray tie. It was somewhat worn, but distinct enough for me to trace the same odd design which had first attracted my eye. This was enough to arouse my strongest suspicions, but whether it was sufficient for the law to take cognizance of I did not consider. My astonishment and the ironical humor of the situation drove everything else out of my mind.

These balls were attended by a great variety of people. They were generally given by the waiters of some one of the big hotels, and were often patronized by a number of hotel guests who came to "see the sights." The crowd was always noisy, but good-natured; there was much quadrille-dancing, and a strong-lunged man called figures in a voice which did not confine itself to the limits of the hall. It is not worth the while for me to describe in detail how these people acted; they conducted themselves in about the same manner as I have seen other people at similar balls conduct themselves. When one has seen something of the world and human nature, one must conclude, after all, that between people in like stations of life there is very little difference the world over.

However, it was at one of these balls that I first saw the cake-walk. There was a contest for a gold watch, to be awarded to the hotel head-waiter receiving the greatest number of votes. There was some dancing while the votes were being counted. Then the floor was cleared for the cake-walk. A half-dozen guests from some of the hotels took seats on the stage to act as judges, and twelve or fourteen couples began to walk for a sure enough, highly decorated cake, which was in plain evidence. The spectators crowded about the space reserved for the contestants and watched them with interest and excitement. The couples did not walk round in a circle, but in a square, with the men on the inside. The fine points to be considered were the bearing of the men, the precision with which they turned the corners, the grace of the women, and the ease with which they swung around the pivots. The men walked with stately and soldierly step, and the women with considerable grace. The judges arrived at their decision by a process of elimination. The music and the walk continued for some minutes; then both were stopped while the judges conferred; when the walk began again, several couples were left out. In this way the contest was finally narrowed down to three or four couples. Then the excitement became intense; there was much partisan cheering as one couple or another would execute a turn in extra elegant style. When the cake was finally awarded, the spectators were about evenly divided between those who cheered the winners and those who muttered about the unfairness of the judges. This was the cake-walk in its original form, and it is what the colored performers on the theatrical stage developed into the prancing movements now known all over the world, and which some Parisian critics pronounced the acme of poetic motion.

There are a great many colored people who are ashamed of the cake-walk, but I think they ought to be proud of it. It is my opinion that the colored people of this country have done four things which refute the oft-advanced theory that they are an absolutely inferior race, which demonstrate that they have originality and artistic conception, and, what is more, the power of creating that which can influence and appeal universally. The first two of these are the Uncle Remus stories, collected by Joel Chandler Harris, and the Jubilee songs, to which the Fisk singers made the public and the skilled musicians of both America and Europe listen. The other two are ragtime music and the cake-walk. No one who has traveled can question the world-conquering influence of ragtime, and I do not think it would be an exaggeration to say that in Europe the United States is popularly known better by ragtime than by anything else it has produced in a generation. In Paris they call it American music. The newspapers have already told how the practice of intricate cake-walk steps has taken up the time of European royalty and nobility. These are lower forms of art, but they give evidence of a power that will some day be applied to the higher forms. In this measure, at least, and aside from the number of prominent individuals the colored people of the United States have produced, the race has been a world influence; and all of the Indians between Alaska and Patagonia haven't done as much.

Just when I was beginning to look upon Jacksonville as my permanent home and was beginning to plan about marrying the young school teacher, raising a family, and working in a cigar factory the rest of my life, for some reason, which I do not now remember, the factory at which I worked was indefinitely shut down. Some of the men got work in other factories in town;

some decided to go to Key West and Tampa, others made up their minds to go to New York for work. All at once a desire like a fever seized me to see the North again and I cast my lot with those bound for New York.

QUESTIONS FOR CRITICAL THINKING AND WRITING

1. What is the significance, according to Johnson's protagonist, of the Parisians referring to ragtime as "American music"?
2. What is the purpose of describing, in great detail, the cake-walk?
3. In the final paragraph of this excerpt, the protagonist explains his desire to move north to New York City. What is the tone of this closing paragraph? Does it give you any indication of the rest of the story?

JEFF KLINKENBERG

Jeff Klinkenberg was born in 1949 in Miami, and he is currently a writer on Florida culture for the *St. Petersburg Times*. In 2008 he published a collection of essays, *Pilgrim in the Land of Alligators*, and in 2007 and 2009, his column "Real Florida" was selected as the best in the nation by the American Association of Sunday Features Editors.

BEFORE YOU READ

Klinkenberg's essay illustrates the collision of nature and humans, and his views fall squarely on nature's side. As you read, take note of why you think Klinkenberg, a self-proclaimed city boy, has such reverence for the natural world. What does he think needs to be done to protect it?

Brooker Creek   *1999*

Hunkered in the sand, I stop to admire the first coyote tracks I have ever seen close. "There seem to be more of them during the last few years," says Craig Huegel, manager of a place called Brooker Creek Preserve. I find it exciting that coyotes have come to my home ground, Pinellas.

Brooker Creek is not the Everglades, nor the Big Cypress, nor the Fakahatchee Strand. It is the wildest place those of us who live in Florida's most urban county have. It has lovely piney woods, shady oak hammocks, magnificent cypress swamps, and wild, wild animals. What I like most about it is the delicious possibility of leaving a trail, hiking into the trees, and getting lost.

Brooker Creek lies east of Tarpon Springs, where Pinellas, Hillsborough, and Pasco counties come together. Outside the 8,000-acre county-owned preserve, progress is running wild. Bulldozers push over trees, cranes dig up the earth, and paving machines make sure highways are smooth and wide. New shopping centers are sprouting along the road like wire grass.

We all know progress is inevitable and, to a degree, welcome. Yet as our world gets more civilized, uncivilized places become even more valuable, especially to those of us destined to live in asphalt jungles.

"We need the tonic of wildness," Thoreau wrote in *Walden*, ". . . to wade sometimes in marshes where the bittern and the meadow-hen lurk, and hear the booming of the snipe, to smell the whispering sedge where only some wilder and more solitary fowl builds her nest, and the mink crawls with its belly close to the ground."

Craig Huegel — his last name rhymes, appropriately, with "eagle" — leads today's expedition accompanied by his friend LaVonne Ries, a volunteer at the preserve. We arrive in Huegel's four-wheel drive vehicle, and when the sand gets deep we walk. Now we hike in the belly of the forest, among the dwarf oaks and the stately pines and tall grass that threatens to devour the modest trail.

I can hardly believe I'm in a county where 3,000 people live per square mile, where traffic tends to be rush-hour bumper to bumper, where boom boxes thump night and day. Our soundtrack is provided by the chattering of gray squirrels and the twittering of rufous-sided towhees.

"I hadn't worked here long when I heard this strange sound," Huegel says, as we walk along. "The sound was coming toward me. I couldn't figure it out. It was the wind coming through the trees. The wind! I knew I'd been living in town too long."

I shudder when I realize how Brooker Creek, considered a prime development area, could have been lost forever. It is easy to shut my eyes and imagine the forest mostly gone and filled with pricey houses, golf courses, and neighborhood shopping centers, the streetlights shining on roads that cover earth where panthers once left tracks.

County residents voted to charge themselves an extra penny of sales tax. The so-called Penny-for-Pinellas helped buy Brooker. Lately the state also has spent tax dollars to add to preserve acreage, through Preservation 2000. Perhaps one day the panthers will appreciate it.

Years ago there were definitely panthers here, and there are people who claim that panthers still travel through the area. State wildlife biologists say Pinellas panthers are unlikely, yet from time to time credible witnesses say they have seen the large, tawny cats with long tails sprint out of the forest, cross the road, and vanish in the woods beyond.

In 1996, Huegel was walking on a preserve road when he discovered what he was sure was a panther track. He made a plaster cast and sent it to state panther experts. The experts said the track belonged to a large dog — a verdict Huegel still doubts. He earned his doctorate studying coyotes, and he knows dog tracks when he sees them.

"I don't think the preserve is large enough to have a panther population or even a bear population," he says, "but who knows? The preserve is surrounded by a lot of open land, and it's possible we could have some large mammals traveling through. I think there may be more panthers in Florida than people know about."

About coyotes there is no doubt. They invaded Florida long ago, and gradually they have worked their way south into Pinellas. Brooker Creek is the only place on which their presence has been documented. Welcome, coyotes.

"They will have an impact on wildlife," Huegel says, "but it's debatable how much of an impact. Some people will disagree with me, but I don't see them becoming a problem, at least here. I'm hoping they'll fill a niche that wolves and panthers once filled—keeping the deer population at a healthy level. I'm hoping they will reduce the fawn crop every year."

Deer tracks dot the sand. So do the tracks of bobcats and foxes. I would love to see the wariest of large birds, the wild turkey. They're here, too.

"Here's a yellow butterwort," Huegel says, bending. We study the beautiful flower. It's a threatened species, but I'm even more excited by longleaf pines. At the turn of the century, they were Florida's dominant pine. Loggers took them first and replanted with faster-growing slash pines. Today, longleaf pines make up only 2 percent of our forests.

Animals that depend on longleafs for life—the red-cockaded woodpecker and the Sherman's fox squirrel—are threatened with extinction. No red-cockaded woodpeckers have been spotted in the preserve, but it is the best place in Pinellas to see fox squirrels. They're substantially bigger than grays, with long graceful tails.

On Saturday mornings, LaVonne Ries and other volunteers lead walking tours of the preserve by reservation only. Sometimes Ries walks slow and short distances, but sometimes, if her guests are fit, she walks long and hard. She is small and lithe and tough. For years she lived on an island that lacked running water and electricity. She feels at home in the preserve, although she carries a compass.

"I've been lost," she says, sounding exhilarated.

Everybody probably should be lost at least once in their life. I have felt lost three times in the Everglades.

Once the airboat on which I was riding broke down deep in the sawgrass at dusk. We knew where we were but knew we wouldn't be found without pushing the boat a long way to a canal. As night arrived, sawgrass cut my torso, and twice I stepped in water over my head, but you're reading these words, so you know my story has a happy ending.

I had another boating mishap in the mangrove section of Everglades National Park. Close to running out of gas, we decided to take a shortcut on the return to Flamingo. Hours later, we had no earthly idea where we were; all mangrove islands do look alike. Fortunately, the only boat we encountered the whole day belonged to a park ranger, who was happy to point the way to the main channel.

A few years ago I went on another wild boating adventure with an Everglades pioneer named Totch Brown. A former commercial fisher and alligator poacher, Totch wanted to show me his favorite old haunts. Some of the creeks were so narrow, and so overgrown, that we had to lie in the boat to pass. Totch was in his seventies and had endured three decades of heart disease. He had a graveyard cough. I clung to my compass.

"Where are we now?" I asked Totch all afternoon, getting him to show me on the charts. If Totch keeled over, could I get us back to Chokoloskee? I enjoyed my day with Totch, but I was relieved when my feet landed on the dock. The Everglades is the largest roadless area in the lower forty-eight states, and I am a city boy.

City boys need the tonic of wildness, and I seem to need it more than most. I don't want to get lost, really, but I like to walk right to the edge of it—just enough to be anxious.

Brooker Creek is not the most beautiful place in Florida, but it belongs to the people of Tampa Bay, and it is wonderful. With additional funding and management, one day it might be a state showpiece.

It is already close to that. Gopher tortoises sit at the mouths of their burrows watching us pass. A rare butterfly, the zebra swallowtail, lands on a paw-paw blossom. Ant lions, hidden at the bottom of little sand depressions, wait for something edible to tumble in.

We leave the trail. We're hiking cross-country now. Craig Huegel seems to know where he is going.

"I did get lost in here," he says. On his first hike, he guided leaders of Pinellas government right into the thigh-deep water of a cypress swamp.

Some people have all the luck.

QUESTIONS FOR CRITICAL THINKING AND WRITING

1. Why does Klinkenberg devote an entire essay to Brooker Creek, even though, as he says, it "is not the most beautiful place in Florida"?

2. What does Klinkenberg believe is the benefit to getting lost, especially in a place like Brooker Creek? What stories does he relate to illustrate his point?

3. Klinkenberg concedes that "progress is inevitable and, to a degree, welcome." Where, then, is the line between progress and conservation drawn, do you think? Does Klinkenberg offer an answer?

4. **CONNECT TO ANOTHER READING.** How does Jeff Klinkenberg's essay compare to Jack Rudloe's "The Elusive Sawfish" (p. 111)? Do the authors share similar beliefs about the interactions of humans and nature?

MADELEINE L'ENGLE

Madeleine L'Engle (1918–2007) is one of the most celebrated and beloved children's writers of the twentieth century. She is the author of *A Wrinkle in Time*, which won the Newbery Medal, and *A Swiftly Tilting Planet*, which won the National Book Award. Although she spent much of her childhood in New York and the French Alps, she moved to South Carolina to finish high school and spent summers in Florida. In total, she wrote more than sixty books.

BEFORE YOU READ

Knowing that Madeleine L'Engle spent many summers in Florida, pay attention to the parallels between the description of the fictional Illyria and that of the coast of Florida. What small details does L'Engle include that are reminiscent of Florida?

From *The Other Side of the Sun* 1971

The air was hot, heavy; new to me. I reached up and closed my fingers as though I could squeeze some of the steaming moisture from the atmosphere. When I got to the beach I sat down on the end of the ramp and took off my shoes and stockings. My feet burned in an acutely painful manner wholly new to me. The physical results of the Illyrian heat were going to take time for me to become accustomed to. I arched my feet, stretched my toes. I could not have stood shoes and stockings a moment longer. I buckled the straps of left and right shoes together, so that I could hang them over my arm. The soft sand at the foot of the ramp was still warm from the sun, and delicious as it sifted between my toes. I moved slowly to the firmer, damper sand at the ocean's edge, then walked along the beautiful coolness close to the sea. As the waves were sucked out into the ocean I could feel a strange suction beneath my feet. Terry had warned me about the tides, the undertow, the treachery lurking beneath the beauty. "Check with Aunt Des about the swimming," he had told me. "She knows the beaches like the palm of her hand, where the undertow is dangerous, where the tide pulls hardest — at least she used to."

I waded up to my ankles in the warm water, the undertow pulling strongly now. I bent down and dabbled my hot hands in the lacy foam. Splattering salt water I moved up the beach, then turned to look back at Illyria.

The old house was set back on the dunes, an extraordinary monstrosity — though I soon came to see it as beautiful — built up on stilts filled in with wooden lattice-work. There were towers and chimneys and wings and elbows and little balconies, and the great, many-angled veranda which surrounded the whole thing like a moat. The dunes raised themselves all about, so that the house seemed to float like an unwieldy ark on a sea of sand. The long wooden ramp, made of the same sea-grey wood as the house, led up from the beach, over a jungle of scrub and wild undergrowth, up onto the veranda.

Oh, Illyria, Illyria. The home place. The place of love. The place where living taught me something about dying, and where death taught me even more about life.

Illyria: always the smell of the sea, of mustiness. Always wind: the wind of the Spirit, even if it sometimes blew in odd nooks and crannies. Wind moving across the face of the water, over the great pale stretch of beach, through the veranda, and into the house, so that the heavy linen damask curtains stirred constantly, rungs undulated, doors slammed.

In the wet sea wind wood swelled. Everything was sticky. Doors were hard to open and close. Shoes left too long unworn became covered with green mold. Little beach ants ate our silk stockings unless we kept them in tightly closed preserving jars. Our clothes were always damp to put on unless they'd just come in out of the sun. In winter nothing dried. Clothes were constantly and ineffectually draped over the fenders, and the smell of warm, damp cloth added itself to the other Illyrian odors.

In the nature of my husband's work with the State Department we were away most of the time, in Africa, China, Rome, St. Petersburg, Paris, London. Our home leaves of course were spent at Illyria, but only our first child, our Theron, was born there, or even in the United States. But Illyria was always home, the place of love — and why? I have been more afraid, more filled with anguish, in Illyria than any place on earth. The answer has something to do with love. Love that has to go through darkness and pain and endurance and a stark acceptance before it can come out into the far light of the sun. Love I hadn't dreamed of, and wouldn't have wanted to dream of, before my husband sent me to Illyria to wait for him.

QUESTIONS FOR CRITICAL THINKING AND WRITING

1. How does L'Engle's physical description of the house and the beach align with the protagonist's statement that Illyria is "The home place. The place of love"?

2. Although this is a short excerpt, it includes many instances of foreshadowing that imply what the tone of the rest of the book will be. Name some of those instances, and describe what they might imply.

3. CONNECT TO ANOTHER READING. Using Madeleine L'Engle's excerpt from *The Other Side of the Sun* and Joan Didion's excerpt from *Miami* (p. 53), discuss the importance of water in Florida. It is ever pervasive and, in both excerpts, seems to develop a personality and motives behind its behavior. Why might water play such an important role in the literature of Florida?

ALTON C. MORRIS

Alton C. Morris (1913–1979) was from the Lake Okeechobee region of Florida. He dedicated his career to the study of Floridian folklore and folksongs and was a professor of folklore at the University of Florida. In 1950 he published his dissertation on Floridian folksongs titled *Folksongs of Florida*, which remains the only collection of its kind.

BEFORE YOU READ

The following three pieces are folksongs, passed down through generations and recorded by Alton C. Morris for preservation. As you read the songs, are you assigning a melody to them or reading them more like poetry? How might the melodies of these songs affect the meaning, and do you think they are as effective written down as they are sung aloud?

The Jolly Bachelor   *1950*

"THE JOLLY BACHELOR." Text furnished by Miss Irene Schmitt, Oxford, who learned the song from her mother, Mrs. F. K. Schmitt, Oxford.

I am a jolly bachelor,
So hearty, hale, and free;
What people want to marry for
Is more than I can see.

Chorus
So now, young ladies,   5
Don't you wait for me,
For I will be a bachelor
So hearty, hale, and free.

I've got a stove that's worth ten cents
A table worth fifteen;   10
I cook my grub in oyster cans
And always keep them clean.

I go to bed whene'er I please;
I get up just the same;
I change my sox three times a year   15
With no one to complain.

And when I die, I go to heaven,
As all good bachelors do;
I will not fret for fear
My wife will get there, too.   20

All My Sins Been Taken Away   *1950*

"Mary Wore Three Silver Chain." Recorded from the singing of Mr. John Richardson, Jacksonville, who learned the song from his father, a native of Alabama.

Mary wore three silver chain;
Oh, Mary wore three silver chain;
Mary wore three silver chain;
Each chain bore the Saviour's name.
All of my sins been taken away, taken away.   5

Oh, Mary weeped, and Martha moaned;
Oh, Mary weeped, and Martha moaned;
Oh, Mary weeped, and Martha moaned;
You better let God's chillun alone.
All of my sins been taken away, taken away.   10

Come and Jine   1950

"COME AND JINE." Text communicated by Miss Geneva Harrell, Apalachicola, who took
it down from the singing of Mrs. Roy Branch, Apalachicola.

There are churches in our land
Run by wicked, worldly men;
They will stand and tell you, brother,
Come and jine!
If you'll only join our crew,   5
You can smoke and drink and chew,
You can be a preacher, too.
Come and jine!

Chorus
Come and jine, the preacher calleth;
Come and jine!   10
You can go to the parties all the time,
If you'll only pay your dues.
You can be a deacon, too.
Come and jine, the preacher calleth;
Come and jine!   15

All the preachers preach for pay;
They'll take fodder, corn, or hay,
But they'll stand and tell you, brother,
Come and jine!
All the members dress as the world   20
With their rubies and their pearls,
But if you start to leave, they'll tell you
Come and jine!

You can do just as you please;
Never get down on your knees,   25
But you must keep on telling the people,
Come and jine!
You can get mad and have a fight,
Or drink liquor till you're tight,
And they'll let you be a full-fledged member   30
All the time.

You can go to picture shows,
And though all the religion oppose,
But you must tell the people,
Come and jine!   35
They will never turn you out
Unless you get religion and begin to shout;
Then they'll tell you to quit that stuff,
Come and jine!

Questions for Critical Thinking and Writing

1. Both "All My Sins Been Taken Away" and "Come and Jine" feature extensive line repetition. What is the result of this repetition, and how does it affect the meaning of the song?

2. How do you interpret "All My Sins Been Taken Away," "The Jolly Bachelor," and "Come and Jine"? Refer to the songs to support your positions.

3. **CONNECT TO ANOTHER READING.** Alton C. Morris was a contemporary of Zora Neale Hurston and worked with her to collect the folksongs he used for his dissertation. In the folksongs, the major themes are marriage and religion, much like in Hurston's story "Sweat" (p. 81). Using both Hurston's story and the folksongs here, write an essay in which you discuss the importance of marriage and religion in Floridian culture and how those themes are reflected in the state's literature and folklore.

Marjorie Kinnan Rawlings

Marjorie Kinnan Rawlings (1896–1953) was a Floridian author best known for her celebrated novel *The Yearling*, about a boy who adopts a fawn, from which this excerpt is taken. The book won the Pulitzer Prize for fiction in 1939 and was adapted into a movie. Rawlings lived in rural Florida and set many of her stories in similar environments.

Courtesy of Bettmann/Corbis.

Before You Read

Rawlings is acclaimed for painting detailed portraits of rural life. As you read, identify how she relates the everyday chores and duties that Jody has. How does Jody handle these chores? How does Jody's daily schedule reflect long-held ideas about rural life?

From *The Yearling*   *1938*

August was merciless in its heat, but it was, mercifully, leisurely. There was little work to be done and no great hurry about the doing of that little. There had been rains and the corn had come to maturity. It was drying on the stalks and could soon be broken for curing. Penny estimated that he would have a good yield, perhaps as much as ten bushels to the acre. The sweet potato vines grew lushly. The Kaffir corn for the chickens was ripening, its long heads like sorghum. The sunflowers along the fence, also for the chickens, had heads as big as plates. The cow-peas were abundant. They made the staple food, with the meat of some game, almost every day. There would be a fine stand of cow-pea hay for use through the winter months. The field of pindars was not doing so well, but because of the killing by old Slewfoot of Betsy the brood sow, there were not many shoats to fatten. The Baxter hogs had come mysteriously home, and with them a young brood sow. Its mark had been changed from the Forrester mark to the Baxter. Penny accepted it as the peace offering for which it was intended.

The red ribbon cane had made a fair stand. The Baxters looked forward to autumn and the frosts, when sweet potatoes would be dug, hogs butchered, corn ground into meal, and the cane would be ground and the juice boiled into syrup, and plenty would replace the meagerness. There was enough to eat, even now in the leanest season, but there was no variety, no richness, no comfortable feeling of ample reserve stores. They lived from day to day, with meal and flour and fat meat short, dependent on Penny's chance shots at deer and turkey and squirrel. He trapped a fat 'possum in the yard one night, and dug a mess of the new sweet potatoes to roast with it, for a special treat. It was an extravagance, for the potatoes were small and immature.

The sun laid a heavy hand on the scrub and on the clearing. Ma Baxter's bulk suffered with the heat. Penny and Jody, lean and clean-limbed, felt the temperature only in an increasing reluctance to move rapidly, or often. They did the chores together in the morning, milked the cow, fed the horse, chopped wood for cooking, brought water from the sink-hole, and then were through until the evening. Ma Baxter cooked hot dinner at noon, then banked the fire on the hearth with ashes; and supper was cold, consisting of the noon surplus.

Jody was conscious always of Fodder-wing's absence. Living, Fodder-wing had been with him, in the back of his mind, a friendly presence to which he might turn in his thoughts, if not in reality. But Flag grew miraculously, day by day, and that was comfort enough. Jody thought that its spots were beginning to fade, a sign of maturity, but Penny could see little change. It was unquestionably growing in intelligence. Penny said that the bears had the largest brains of any of the scrub animals, and the brain of the deer came next.

Ma Baxter said, "This un's too dad-ratted smart," and Penny said, "Why, Ma, shame on you for cussin'," and winked at Jody.

Flag learned to lift the shoe-string latch on the door and come in the house at any hour of the day or night, when he was not shut up. He butted a feather pillow from Jody's bed and tossed it all over the house until it burst, so that feathers drifted for days in every nook and cranny, and appeared from nowhere in a dish of biscuit pudding. He began to romp with the dogs. Old Julia was too dignified to do much more than wag her tail slowly when he pawed at her, but Rip growled and circled and pretended to pounce, and Flag kicked up his heels and flicked his merry tail and shook his head and finally, with impudence, leaped the slat fence and raced alone down the roadway. He liked best to play with Jody. They tussled and held furious butting matches and raced side by side, until Ma Baxter protested that Jody was growing as lean as a black snake.

In a late afternoon toward the end of August, Jody went with the fawn to the sink-hole for fresh water for supper. The road was bright with flowers.

The sumac was in bloom, and the colic root sent up tall stalks of white or orange orchid-like flowers. The French mulberries were beginning to ripen on slim stems. They were lavender in color, close-clustered, like snails' eggs along lily stalks. Butterflies sat on the first purple buds of the fragrant deer-tongue, opening and closing their wings slowly, as though waiting for the buds to open and the nectar to be revealed. The covey call of quail sounded again from the pea-field, clear and sweet and communal. Sunset was coming a little earlier, and at the corner of the fence-row, where the old Spanish trail turned north and passed the sink-hole, the saffron light reached under the low-hanging live oaks and made of the gray pendulous Spanish moss a luminous curtain.

Jody stopped short with his hand on the fawn's head. A horseman with a helmet was riding through the moss. Jody took a step forward, and horse and rider vanished, as though their substance were no thicker than the moss. He stepped back and they appeared again. He drew a long breath. Here, certainly, was Fodder-wing's Spaniard. He was not sure whether he was frightened or no. He was tempted to run back home, telling himself that he had truly seen a spirit. But his father's stuff was in him, and he forced himself to walk forward slowly to the spot in which the apparition had appeared. In a moment the truth was plain. A conjunction of moss and limbs had created the illusion. He could identify the horse, the rider and the helmet. His heart thumped with relief, yet he was disappointed. It would be better not to have known; to have gone away, believing.

He continued on to the sink-hole. The sweet bay was still in bloom, filling the sink-hole with its fragrance. He longed for Fodder-wing. Now he should never know whether the mossy horseman in the sunset was the Spaniard, or whether Fodder-wing had seen yet another, at once more mystic and more true. He set down his buckets and went down the narrow trail that Penny had cut between banks to the floor of the sink-hole, long before he was born.

He forgot his errand and lay down under the lacy shadow of a dogwood tree at the foot of the slope. The fawn nosed about, then lay down beside him. He could see from this spot the whole deep-sunk bowl at once. The rim above caught the glow of the sunset, as though a ring of fires burned invisibly around it. Squirrels, quieted a moment by his coming, began to bark and chatter and swing across the tree-tops, frenzied with the last hour of day, as they were always frenzied with the first. The palm fronds made a loud rattling where they dashed through, but the live oaks gave almost no record of their passing. In the thick sweet gums and hickories they were almost inaudible, always unseen, until they raced up and down the tree trunks or slipped to the edge of a limb to swing into another tree. Birds made sweet sharp sounds in the branches. Far away, a red-bird sang richly, coming closer and closer, until Jody saw him drift to the Baxter drinking trough. A flock of turtle doves whirred in, to drink briefly, then flew away to their roosting places in the adjoining pine forest. Their wings whistled, as though their pointed gray and rosy feathers were thin knives to slash the air.

Jody's eye caught a motion at the edge of the slope. A mother raccoon came down to the limestone troughs, followed by two young ones. She fished the series of troughs carefully, beginning with the drinking trough at the upper level. He had the finest reason now for delaying. He would have to wait until the water had cleared and settled. The mother 'coon found nothing of interest in the troughs. One of the young clambered to the edge of the stock-trough and peered in curiously. She slapped it away, out of danger. She worked her way down the slope. Now she was lost among the tall ferns. Now her black-masked face appeared again between stalks of the Cherokee bean. The two young ones peered out after her, their small faces replicas of her own, their bushy tails ringed almost as decisively.

She reached the seepage pool at the bottom and began to fish in earnest. Her long black fingers groped under fallen twigs and branches. She lay on her side to reach into a crevice for, no doubt, a crayfish. A frog jumped and she made a quick circular pounce and waded back to the edge with it. She sat up on her hind legs and held it a moment, kicking, against her breast, then sunk her teeth in it and shook it, as a dog shakes a rat. She dropped it between her off-spring. They pounced on it and snarled and growled and cracked its bones and finally shared it. She watched dispassionately a moment, then turned back into the pool. Her bushy tail was lifted just above the water level. The young ones waded out after her. Their peaked noses lifted above the water. She turned and saw them and dragged them back to land. She lifted each one in turn and spanked its small furry bottom in so human a way that Jody had to clap his hand over his mouth to keep from shouting. He watched her for a long time, fishing and feeding them. Then she ambled leisurely across the floor of the sink-hole and up the far slope and away over the rim, the young ones following, chirring and grumbling amiably together.

The sink-hole lay all in shadow. Suddenly it seemed to Jody that Fodder-wing had only now gone away with the raccoons. Something of him had been always where the wild creatures fed and played. Something of him would be always near them. Fodder-wing was like the trees. He was of the earth, as they were earthy, with his gnarled, frail roots deep in the sand. He was like the changing clouds and the setting sun and the rising moon. A part of him had been always outside his twisted body. It had come and gone like the wind. It came to Jody that he need not be lonely for his friend again. He could endure his going.

He went to the drinking trough and filled the buckets with as much water as he could carry, and went home. He told at table of the 'coons, and even his mother was interested to hear about the spanking, and no one questioned his delay. After supper, he sat with his father and listened to the hoot-owls and the frogs, and a far wild-cat and still further foxes, and to the north, a wolf that howled and was answered. He tried to tell his father the thing that he had felt that day. Penny listened gravely, and nodded, but Jody could not make the words fit his feeling, and could not quite make his father understand.

QUESTIONS FOR CRITICAL THINKING AND WRITING

1. What is Jody's relationship with the fawn? How does Rawlings effectively convey the relationship in the space of this short excerpt?

2. How does Jody relate to his father in this excerpt? Is his father supportive or dismissive, and what kind of environment does Jody live in? Cite specific passages that support your statements.

3. In the last paragraph, Jody tries to relate to his father that "thing that he had felt that day." What is it that he felt, and why was it so profound?

J. RUSSELL REAVER

J. Russell Reaver was born in Phoenixville, Pennsylvania, in 1915. He was inspired by the folklore and musical traditions of his ancestors, who were Pennsylvania Dutch and Quaker, and became a scholar of folklore. After joining the faculty at Florida State University in the early 1950s, Reaver taught the university's first folklore course, and he used his time in Florida to research and write specifically about Floridian folklore. Shortly before his death in 2002, he received the Florida Folk Heritage Award.

BEFORE YOU READ

Consider some of the common themes that have appeared in folklore you have heard or studied previously. What are those themes, and are they represented in these stories? Why might folklore from different regions have similar themes?

Larger Than Life   *1987*

"Well, I was a night watchman," said Mack. "I was a pretty good watchman, too. Never went to sleep much. But this night I was tired and kind of dozed off and got to dreaming about falling off the bridge into the water. That woke me up with a start, when I hit the water in my dream. Anyway, when I woke up, I found I had kicked my lantern off the bridge into the water. I looked down and could kind of see a faint glimmer, but I wasn't fixing to go down and retrieve it.

"Some five or six years later, I was fishing off that same bridge in about the same place where I kicked my lantern over. Well, I felt something heavy on my line when I went to bring it up. So I pulled and pulled and got it up, and I'll be damned if it wasn't that lantern still burning."

A neighbor named Martin was sitting nearby and couldn't let Mack's story go unchallenged. He said, "About a month ago I went fishing down in the Gulf. We were about ten miles out when I set up my lines. Saw one of them kind of quiver, so I pulled it in, and on the hook was a beautiful ten-pound freshwater bass."

One of the onlookers who hadn't opened his mouth the whole time exclaimed, "You old fellows are getting too old to tell all those lies. Better be making peace with your Maker instead of making the devil smile."

To which Mack replied, "If he'll knock ten pounds off his fish, I'll blow out my lantern. . . ."

Rain   *1987*

"In any place where there is much rain, stories or good-natured slams will be told about it. On a rainy day here in Tallahassee I heard this story.

"One time a very bad storm was coming up and it looked like once the rain started it would never stop. A farmer looked up and saw the sky and immediately called his hired man in. He told him that they were really going to profit by the rain this time. The farmer told the hired man that the cow they had butchered the last fall was in their deep freeze. 'What I want you to do,' the farmer said, 'is to get those two sides of beef and put a little chunk of it on each of the barbs on our barbed-wire fence. From what I counted as we put up the fence, you will find 900,000 barbs out here, so you had better get to work right now.'

"Well, that hired man went and got the beef and started his job and just finished it before the storm broke. He came rushing back to the farm house and he and the farmer sat together and watched the rain come down. It rained for days and days and finally the land could absorb no more water, so it started flooding. The water rose higher and higher and finally their whole farming area was flooded, and the barbed-wire fence was completely covered. The hired man still couldn't figure out why he had put the beef out there. Well, in due course of time the water receded and as it did so, it was possible to see that on each barb on the fence there was a fish. They ran out and started bringing in the fish and when they finished the farmer started counting them. Then, in a rage, he fired the hired man. You see, there were 900,000 barbs and they had just caught 899,999 fish."

More Stretchers   1987

a. "A man killed a mosquito so big that he fenced in ten acres of land with the bones. In the field he planted corn and raised ten barrels to the acre. He housed it all in the mosquito's skull."

b. "A man planted a watermelon vine in a swamp. It grew a melon so big that he had to make a ladder three hundred feet high to cut it from the stem. The watermelon burst, and there was so much water in it that they put up a water mill and ground three hundred bushels of corn with the juice."

c. "The mosquitoes were so bad one night that a man crawled under a hundred-gallon sugar kettle to keep them from biting him. The mosquitoes were so big and tough that they bit right through the iron kettle. The man braided their bills on the inside of the pot. He braided so many and they were so strong that they flew off with the kettle."

d. *The Big Pumpkin*

"A farmer who lived deep in a swamp planted one hundred ninety-two acres of land in pumpkins. One hundred ninety-two hills came up, but the cutworms ate down all but one hill. It grew one hundred ninety-two pumpkins, but a goat got onto the field an' stomped off all but one. This 'un grew so big that it pushed the fences down all around the field.

"This same farmer had a sow and nine pigs. One day he lost them, and he hunted and hunted. Still he couldn't find the pigs. He asked everyone, but no one had seen them.

"On the twenty-eight of March, the man heard a terrible racket in the side of his field. He went down to the field, and there was his sow and pigs rollin' out pumpkin seeds. He saw his pumpkin had a big hole in it; so he stuck his head inside. And, gentlemen! Know what he saw? There on one side of the pumpkin was ten cows and ten calves, and they had all gnawed a stall out of the pumpkin meat. The pigs and sow had been staying in the pumpkin too.

"The farmer sold his sow and pigs for a hundred and ninety-two dollars and gave all his neighbors seed to plant so that they could raise a pumpkin as big as his."

e. *The Peachy Deer*

"One day a man decided to go hunting, but he didn't have any ammunition. He wanted to go huntin' real bad; so he decided to use peach seeds for bullets. Pretty soon he saw a big buck. He shot the deer with the peach seed and hit him in the side, but didn't kill him. The hunter had to go home without any game. The peach seed, when it went in the deer's side, started sprouting. The sprouts forked; one branch came out each of the deer's antlers.

"The ole man got crippled and had to stay in bed for four years. As soon as he got up, he got bullets for his rifle and went back to the woods where he had shot the deer.

"When he entered the woods, he saw a peach on the ground; so he picked it up and ate it. Pretty soon he saw another; he picked it up and put it in his pocket. He kept findin' them and his pockets got full. He heard a sound and looked up. There before him was the biggest buck he had ever seen, with two full-grown peach trees, full of peaches, growing out of his ears."

f. *The Three Sons*

"An ole man had three boys. He was a poor ole man, who had no money and just a small place. One day he said to the boys, 'Boys, I ain't got nuthin' but this place. I want each of you to get me sompun' good to eat. The one who brings the best thing to eat will get the place.' The only things the ole man had to give the boys to help them was fish hooks, a gun, a knife, three shells, and one ole dog.

"The baby boy took the fish hooks, and he soon brought in a big red-breast perch. The ole man was mighty pleased, 'cause he liked perch. Looked like the baby boy was going to get the place; but the middle-sized boy came in with a big shoat. He had taken the knife and dressed the shoat, and it looked like fine pork. If there was anything the ole man liked better than perch, it was good pork.

"The ole man said to the oldest boy, 'Son, little boy brought in perch, and the middle boy brought pork. Don't reckon you can beat them. Guess one of them gets the place.' But the oldest boy took the gun, the three shells, and Ole Ring, the dog, and went hunting. First he found a squirrel. He shot it, but it wasn't fine enough to take his pa. Next he saw a turkey gobbler, and he shot it too. This left him with only one shell.

"He went on a little piece further, and Ring started pointing at a cat-faced stump. The boy saw a doe lying on one side of the stump and a buck on the other. He started to raise his rifle to shoot them when he remembered he had only one shell. So he got his knife out and sez, 'Catch 'em, Ring!' The dog jumped and hit the stump head on. The dog split himself into two pieces; one piece hit the buck and the other hit the doe. While they were stunned, the boy jumped on them and cut their throats. Then he put the two halves of the dog together and rubbed his hands over them. Ole Ring run 'round good as new.

"When the oldes' boy took the squirrel, the turkey, and two deer home, his paw gave him the place, for as his pa sez, 'If there's anything I like better 'un fish er pork, it's good ole venzun.'"

QUESTIONS FOR CRITICAL THINKING AND WRITING

1. What role does food play in many of these tales? Why might it recur so often, even in this small sampling? Use specific examples to illustrate your point.

2. What are the major differences in the morals of a tale like "Larger Than Life" versus those in a tale like "The Three Sons"? What aspects of a community or society might these different kinds of tales represent?

3. What specific folklore or tall tales have you heard in your past that remind you of these? Choose one tale that you are familiar with and compare and contrast it with one of Reaver's tales. Are the morals, characters, or outcomes similar?

JACK RUDLOE

Jack Rudloe was born in New York City in 1943. Today, he is a well-known American nature writer, focusing on studying and protecting marine species, and is also active in the fight to save the disappearing Florida wetlands. Poet James Dickey said of the author, "If any of the creatures in earth, water, air, or fire continue to survive, Jack Rudloe and his brothers in visionary conservation will be looked on as saints: saviors not only of humanity, but of the living planet itself."

Courtesy of Jack Rudloe.

BEFORE YOU READ

Many of the authors in this book discuss the balance of nature versus humans in Florida. Jack Rudloe is often forced to choose between profit and the preservation of nature. As you read, think about how Rudloe justifies his actions.

The Elusive Sawfish   *1988*

As our fiberglass boat bounced over the chop, heading out into the Gulf off Carrabelle, I sat somberly on the stern holding the ashes of a friend, a man who had spent his life on the sea or trying to get to it. This was obviously not a routine collecting trip, although we were going out to look for barnacles on ropes of abandoned crab traps. Elwood A. Curtis wouldn't have it any other way. In his book, *A Wet Butt and Hungry Gut,* he detailed his life on shrimp boats and snapper boats, describing a Florida of fifty years ago that I had never known, a time when panthers roamed the beaches and crews of hungry beach seiners dragged manatees up onto the shores and ate them. He had nearly starved trying to become a commercial fisherman and had ended up selling ads and doing other unrelated jobs.

Always he gravitated back to the water, someplace where there were grass beds with sea trout and sandbars, where the redfish gathered. Old and sick, he spent his last days fishing on docks, messing around oyster shoals, and wading out into the marshes. And it was his last wish that he be cremated and his ashes scattered at sea.

Ahead, at the far end of the channel, the turbid waters broke on a sandbar, and its yellow shallows rose up from the sea bottom. I directed Doug Gleeson, our chief collector, to run the boat in that direction.

I sat on the stern, next to our scallop dredge and buckets and the little velvet box that contained the ashes of a man who had loved the sea. A stiff wind was blowing, making the water choppy, and pushing in the tide, giving it the appearance of the rolling ocean. Today it was the south wind blowing, pushing saltier and bluer water over the tide flats. The Gulf of Mexico had moved in on top of the estuary, with rolling swells and whitecaps and a refreshing stiff breeze.

It was time to unpack my friend. I opened the sealed box and pulled out the can that held the cremated remains. Strange, I thought, here was a human being I had known and talked to only a few months ago, and now he was ashes. I pried it open, and looked with a morbid fascination at the white crushed bones and dust packed so densely inside. It looked like seashells, not much different from the rubble that lined the bottom of the channel or was cast up on the barrier beaches in fragments and shards. Simple calcium carbonate, the fabric of life, just like the limestone and the foraminifers.

There was nothing to say, no ceremony, for the sea said it all. I motioned Doug to slow down and putter along the edge of the shoal, and I up-ended the can. The white bones poured out, and the dust took to the air. I watched the heavy particles sinking down through the waves, spinning, churning like pennies falling down a wishing well, down to the brittle stars below, down to the speckled sea trout he loved so much, the shrimp, the squid — life, abundant life.

I put the can and wrappings overboard too. A purist might cry pollution, but I figured the sea could handle it. A toadfish or stone crab would probably make its home in it, and Curt would approve of that.

Suddenly, my philosophical ruminations were interrupted by Doug's cry, "Hey, look at that!"

He was pointing to a large, flat shape moving slowly on top of the sandbar. He speeded up and headed for the elongated brown carpetlike creature that moved like a shadow. Even from the distance, it was obviously some kind of ray, but it was huge. Three triangular fins broke the surface, big, brown, and rough, like sandpaper. It was a sawfish, one that was easily ten feet long, a rare sight. It stopped and squatted on the bottom, and we watched it in all its awesome size. Doug throttled down the motor, and we puttered forward to get a better look.

What a great reward for scattering my friend's ashes, I thought. It was a gift just to see it. I regarded the sawfish as a harbinger of good fortune, as the Japanese shark fishermen consider the hammerhead shark a messenger from the god of the sea.

Before I made the trip, I reread his book and chuckled at his recollections of catching a sawfish and peddling its bill to the tourists in a Jensen Beach bar.

There must be some inherent reason that mantelpieces around the world are adorned with the stuffed trophies of sword-bearing fish. Most of those fighting marlins, sailfish, and occasional swordfishes look more like replicas popped out of a manufacturer's plastic injection mold than the living creatures they once were. Perhaps we make trophies of sawfishes and swordfish because of some inherent fascination with the sword. Excalibur, King Arthur's legendary sword, is ingrained in our mythology, a story told down through the ages. What better feeling is there than to hold a well-balanced rapier in one's hand?

I watched the lightest dust particles of Curt's ashes float away on the surface, rising and falling with the waves as we turned back to shore. I knew the Creator, who cooked up the whole mess in the first place, used some of the same ingredients to make both man and billfish.

Every year people spend millions of dollars to go out and catch these streamlined masterpieces. The billfishes are true fish, with bony skeletons, that inhabit the open oceans. Commercial long-liners travel the Gulf Stream from the Caribbean to Canada in search of these hydrodynamic wonders that think nothing of speeding from six-hundred-foot depths up to the surface to strike bait and skewer it on their rapiers. They have a tight network of blood vessels surrounding their brains that enables them to function in great depths, keeping their brains and bodies warm. Swordfish feed down in the depths on squid and then rise to the warmer waters of the surface to digest their meals.

Although the sawfish is a peaceful animal, and has never deliberately attacked anyone except when harpooned or caught in nets or on hook and line, there are records of swordfishes ramming swords up through the bottom of boats, and even a few people meeting an end with a spear in their bellies. The submersible *Ben Franklin* encountered a swordfish. They were drifting six hundred feet below the surface following the Gulf Stream in 1969 when they were surprised by an assault. Their log entry read,

> It was really an attack, short, precise. The swordfish was about five or six feet long. Another one was waiting for him at the limit of our visibility. The combatant rushed forward and apparently tried to hit our porthole, missing it by a few inches. Then he circled around several minutes close to the boat. Content that his domination of this portion of his realm was not threatened, he joined his friend and left, never to be seen again. What courage for such a fish to take on a 130-ton submarine.

The smaller sailfish have been photographed off the east coast of Florida herding swarms of pilchards, little herringlike fishes, together in a tight bunch and skewering them. "Balling the bait," it's called. With their long fanlike dorsal fins raised to make them look even larger, they continually circle the panicked, glittering little silver fishes forcing them into a tight mass, almost like sardines in a can. Then they come crashing in, a nightmare of spears, leaving the maimed and wounded bait fish to sink, swooping down and swallowing them whole. They whittle away at the packed mass of little fish until it becomes smaller and smaller. Meanwhile, sport fishermen cruise above, snatching their lines and lures, reeling up the fighting billfish one right after the other, until the wind switches, the seas become choppy, and the minnows disperse along with the sailfish.

The sawfish, *Pristis pectinatus*, does not frequent the open ocean, as billfish do; it is a creature of coastal waters, river mouths, estuaries, and sandbars. Its saw is very different from the sharp, pointed rapier of the billfish. It is a large flat blade with lateral rows of protruding toothlike spikes. Exactly what it uses its vorpal sword for isn't really known, and there is some dispute about it. Sawfish are said to swim through a school of small fish, making hard lateral sweeps, impaling some on their saws, and leaving the hacked-up mutilated bodies of others to tumble to the bottom, where they swallow them whole. Some ichthyologists doubt this and believe the toothy rostrum is really used to root clams and worms out of the sand. But for all we know, it may also be an elaborate antenna for picking up electrical fields in the ocean as well.

The sawfish is so rare that virtually nothing is known about its natural history. I watched this large prime specimen heading for deeper water and freedom with mixed feelings. On the one hand, I wanted to see it go free, to procreate, and make more sawfish, and hoped it would slip past the phalanx of commercial fishermen's nets and the lines of anglers. But there also went a valuable creature, much in demand by oceanariums. Two hundred dollars a delivered foot was cruising over the shallow sand bottom like a great moving carpet. We needed the money to pay salaries and support the laboratory, and therein lay the conflict. I saw nothing wrong with collecting marine invertebrates and fish that rapidly recolonize the environment and produce copious offspring. We essentially were one more predator that did not impact the population. But a slow-growing sawfish might be different; it might leave a gap.

The sawfish does not appear on any endangered species list, neither are there laws against catching one. They are not listed as "rare" or "threatened," but perhaps they should be. They seemed far rarer now than when I began working on the Gulf Coast. As I watched it move, I was glad I didn't have a net on board.

The sawfish must have read my avaricious mind and speeded up. Its triangular tail swished back and forth, propelling the long flattened body toward the deeper water. And just before it disappeared I had a wild thought of leaping on it, tackling it, and dragging it into the boat. But fear and common sense, and some firsthand experience with the saw, kept me from it. Twenty years ago in Madagascar it was only by a whisker that I wasn't maimed or killed by a blow from a twenty-foot sawfish.

As part of their cultural and scientific programs, the French government in cooperation with the Malagasy Republic were instituting a fisheries program.

The research vessel *Ambariaka* traveled around the northern coast of Madagascar taking oceanographic measurements of salinity, dissolved oxygen, and temperature and gathering plankton samples. In addition to two French technicians, the crew consisted of six Sakalava natives and five Comorians, who worked on the grounds of the Centre d'Oceanographie. In addition to cutting grass and performing maintenance jobs, they sorted plankton and were trained to take oceanographic measurements. As a participant of the International Indian Ocean Expedition, I was invited to make the maiden shrimping voyage of the vessel because of my background of shrimping in the Gulf of Mexico.

To my knowledge no one had ever shrimped the northwest coast of Madagascar. Years later it was to become a booming shrimp grounds, but until then no net had ever churned the bottom. With too many hands helping, we spread out the net, fed it out behind the R/V *Ambariaka* until it stretched wide like a proper funnel. Then we hoisted the doors over the side with Michon, a French technician, translating my suggestions; held them by the towropes until they spread the net; and allowed it to sink.

In a few moments the little diesel-powered boat came tight on the ropes, and we were fishing virgin bottoms. The *Ambariaka* strained ahead, towing the heavy nets, chains, and doors. I could feel the wind blowing hard in our faces, and the boat began to rock. Soon the wind picked up even more, and the sky darkened, heavy with rain clouds, and lightning flashed on the shoreline followed by a clap of thunder. We all got into our raincoats and held on.

Hollering, "Heave, heave, heave—ho!" the crew hauled back the ropes, piling them up on deck. With much groaning, they lifted the heavy doors up out of the water.

The net was gorged. I grabbed the webbing along with everyone else and hauled back with all my might. I felt the cords of crisscrossed nylon cutting into my fingers as I lifted my share and inched the wings up. Again, I wished I had a real shrimp boat with a real winch and hoisting equipment out here.

But sixteen strong backs and hands can do their share, and the mouth of the net emerged. Feeling seasick, and being less attentive than I should have been, I bent over and looked down into the mouth of the great funnel. And there was a large pair of primordial yellow eyes staring back at me, a great raylike creature. What was that thing?

At the same instant something jolted me; something sharp and exceedingly painful slammed into my shoulder. The pain was excruciating. I glanced at my side, saw what had caused the blow, a huge brown tooth-studded saw sticking straight up from the webbing, and I jumped backward just as it made another swipe.

The crew went wild, yelling, gesticulating, and pointing to the monster in the net. It was a huge sawfish, the largest thing I had ever seen. And it had clobbered me. How fortunate I was that its saw was heavily wrapped up in the webbing, impeded from getting up much of a sideways thrust. Looking at those rows of two-inch-long teeth, rising up and out of the net, I knew how close I had come to being killed.

Two of the crew members had seen me absorb the blow and, with a look of concern in their eyes, asked how I was. There was no need of translations here. "*C'est bon*," I said, shrugging it off. "No problem."

I didn't want anybody to say a thing about the stupidity of my sticking my head and shoulder down into the net. With my shoulder throbbing, I backed away as they went on hauling up the net by hand. They had a block and tackle wrapped around the fish and were groaning and straining and hoisting it out an inch at a time. Fearfully I unbuttoned my shirt and looked. I saw a series of ugly red marks up and down my arm. The skin was broken, and the pain was terrible, but the wounds weren't deep and I would recover to tell the story.

At last they got the sawfish up on deck, still encased in the net. It instantly went wild, thrashing around, slamming its saw back and forth into the mast, the deck, everywhere.

We were thankful that most of it was still encased in the net. Disaster could occur at any moment. At one point, its big brown sandpapery tail bowled over a crewman and sent him sprawling across the deck.

He responded with a quick fury, grabbing a club and delivering a crushing blow to the sawfish's head, which caused it to gyrate even more frantically. Captain LaBarse ordered everyone to get away from it, so it could die and we could safely approach the rest of the catch in the net. Sadly, it took a long time to die, feebly moving its huge body, its yellow belly turning red and hemorrhaging, as its life slowly passed away. Finally, the saw was lashed to the mast. The drama ended.

I had forgotten entirely about being seasick, but now that the drama was over, I was beginning to feel wretched again.

For hours, as we worked through the night, I felt that we had somehow offended the god of the sea by destroying such a creature and at one point suggested that we throw it back. "Oh no!" the French scientists said. "No one has ever seen such a big sawfish before. The saw will make a fine trophy for our museum."

I thought of the Malagasy's belief in propitiating the various gods of the sea, such as the dugong, the whale, and sea turtles, to render fishing favorable. Theirs was an animistic religion, and having watched this great creature expire, I felt we had violated some taboo. But as the net was coming up again, and I had seasickness to fight and specimens to take back to the Smithsonian, I soon forgot about the huge creature.

Suddenly there was a hot burnt smell coming from the engine. Down in the motor hole the pounding pistons began to labor and wheeze and sputter. Black smoke poured out of the stack where only a continuous puff of gray smoke filtered out before. Two crewmen rushed down the ladder to the small engine room to check the gauges. The temperature had soared to two hundred degrees.

Captain LaBarse immediately ordered the engine shut down. For a moment we drifted, with only the creaking sounds of a hot engine. "Has the *Ambariaka* ever had this problem before?" I asked.

"No, never," replied Michon. There were only silence and quick exchanges of knowing looks among the crew in the dim light.

Even if I couldn't see it, I could feel the barren teeth of the mountainous landscape, the mangroves, and the bleakness out there in those sharky waters where monsters like this sawfish cruise the shallows. Although the stench of diesel made me retch, I followed Michon down into the engine room and looked at the mechanical heart of the vessel. The water had been circulating rapidly through the engine; there was no apparent blockage of the cooling system. The motor had been sputtering as if the fuel filters were clogged, but when opened, they appeared to be fine. The engine had used a quart of oil, but there was no sign that anything was drastically wrong.

While we were waiting for the engine to cool down, I inquired, "What happens if we get stranded out here?"

LaBarse shrugged. "I am not sure. We might have to run the boat up on the shore, get out, and hike back to the Center, but it's a long way." Looking at it from a mile or two offshore, I could imagine slogging through that muck, crawling in and out of the tangle of mangrove roots with clouds of mosquitoes devouring us.

"There is a village twenty-five miles back. From there we could get a pirogue and proceed another twenty miles or so to the Centre d'Oceanographie," Monsieur Michon said.

I held on and gazed at the bleak mountainous coast of northwest Madagascar. The shoreline looked burned, uninviting, inhospitable. It was by far the most desolate and remote shoreline I had seen, a land of erosion where the rains washed the red clay mountains into the muddy Mozambique Channel. Mile after mile of dense, thick mangrove swamps covered the shoreline, mangroves full of crocodiles and hungry sharks. A lot to look forward to!

At last we cranked the engine, but the clatter was not reassuring. The Comorian engineer and a helper stayed down in the engine room, squirting oil on every moving part and keeping a constant eye on the temperature gauge. The engineer was sweating and half-asphyxiated, but with great dedication he nurtured the ailing engine.

And so the *Ambariaka* with its giant sawfish clattered along slowly, a full ten hours back to the Centre d'Oceanographie. We never had to make that trek through the mangroves, but cutting the trip short was quite a setback. I had limited time in Madagascar and had to return with a load of specimens. Save for a few small sharks, and a handful of invertebrates, all we retrieved was the sawfish. The crew of the *Ambariaka* were treated as conquering heroes with this incredible twenty-foot monster, a relic from the strange world of the distant past.

With great ceremony the creature was measured and photographed for the museum's records before the admiring eyes of the French scientists' families and the staff at the Centre d'Oceanographie. The severed bill alone measured seven feet with its two rows of three-inch-long spikes. Everyone passed it around, admiring its weight, and a few of the natives performed a fearsome war dance with it, swinging it about against imaginary opponents. The same design has been used in warfare before. The Aztecs made swords that looked just like the sawfish's blade by embedding sharp spikes of black obsidian along a flat board. Had the idea been inspired by one of these great creatures?

The crew of the *Ambariaka* were given the meat, and they divided it up for their families and for selling in the marketplace. I was offered a large chunk, but turned it down. Over the years since I have tried sawfish. Various books laud their flavor and say how prized young sawfish are. I'm afraid I've always found it much too strong, full of urea. It can be made to taste edible, but it takes work that isn't worth the effort.

Because of the confusion between swordfish and sawfish, more than a few people have been duped into buying sawfish meat. But, as one fish peddler found out, it is a far cry from the succulent flesh of the big sleek oceanic swordfishes broiled with lemon-and-butter sauce. Once a fourteen-foot sawfish was caught in a shrimp net and hauled to the dock at Panacea. There it hung, halfway up the mast of the trawler, its great girth pressing down on the ropes, cutting into its flesh. After everyone came by and took photographs and cut off the saw, the shrimpers were mulling over what to do with it. If they threw it overboard, it would rot and stink up the dock. Yet they didn't want to go to all the trouble of untying the boat and hauling the carcass out into the channel.

And then a miracle happened. A fish peddler who was new to the business came by. Seeing this great prize he jumped at the chance and offered the fishermen three dollars a pound for the dressed meat and fifty dollars for the saw. Happily they butchered it and loaded baskets full of meat into his truck.

The peddler promptly paid them over three hundred dollars and sped off with the meat to an exclusive restaurant to offer them fresh swordfish. It was put on the menu as a special. But a few days later the irritated fish peddler angrily returned to the docks, having been berated by the restaurant and forced to take back all the uncooked meat. He learned the hard way the difference between elasmobranchs, the rays and sharks having a cartilaginous skeleton, and the teleosts, the bony fish that include billfish that do not accumulate urea in their body tissues.

As the years passed, I saw fewer and fewer sawfish. They move too slowly to outrun shrimp trawls, and their toothy blades tangle up in almost any size of gill net. And no sport fisherman will turn one loose when he catches a sawfish on a hook and line. It's considered to be an international game fish, though I don't know why. The legend and confusion that sawfish are good eating — not that people who say it have ever tried one — persist along the Gulf Coast.

Several months later, Johnnie and Edward Keith, two of my best collectors, came driving through the gate, blowing their horn, with two six-foot sawfish in the back. Then came my dilemma. If I were a real purist I would have refused to buy them. Or if I were rich, I would have paid them for their struggle to keep them alive, after they caught them in the gill net, loaded them into the boat, then turned the fish loose after tagging them.

Instead, I was happy to get the pair and hurried to make room for them in our tanks. As we slid them into our largest tank, and watched the big toothy rays swim around the circumference, exploring the boundaries, I rationalized that it was really a big ocean, that we really didn't know whether the scarcity in recent years were a function of a reduced population or some long-range environmental change such as a change in the Gulf Stream, a shift in the magnetic flux of the earth's field, sunspots, or any one of a thousand other variables that often regulate fish populations.

As we watched the two sawfish settle down, Johnnie and Edward recounted how they struck a school of mullet, never dreaming there was anything unusual going on. And when the net began jerking and snatching, they knew they had something big. Moments later when a severely tangled saw popped up, they knew what it was. The big surprise was the second sawfish. Knowing they were valuable, and hoping to lessen damage, they cut the ball of webbing away from their bills. Thus they freed the saws by severely damaging their net.

As I watched the sawfish on the bottom of my tank, slowly, rhythmically moving their gills, swimming now and then and stopping, I wondered whether they were a mated pair. The large one was a male, with two long claspers hanging down behind the anal vent, and the other lacked them, thus was a female. Part of me said they should be out there in the ocean, making more sawfish. Another part said that in this age of asphalt and need for environmental sensitivity, it was better that people get a chance to see and appreciate these incredible wonders behind the glass walls of an aquarium. Seeing them alive would be a once-in-a-lifetime experience. And maybe, just maybe, they would give birth, and the aquarium could raise them up and release the surplus young into the wild. The only hope for many endangered species of reptiles, birds, and mammals is captive rearing. Why not rear such fish?

Of course, I knew that I was putting forth a biased argument. The truth was that I was going to sell them to the highest bidder, and that made all my rational arguments suspect. I kept all this concern to myself. After all the trouble my collectors went to, I didn't think they would appreciate hearing it. Another part of me said that this was a great gift from nature, from God or the Great Turtle Mother and I should rejoice—probably the same thing the caveman said as he hurled his spear into the now extinct woolly mastodon and the North American camel.

Several days later we were preparing to ship them to the New York Aquarium. Nixon Griffis really wanted a deep-water sawshark, a creature from seven hundred fathoms. The curator in charge of the exhibits was delighted with the idea of receiving not one, but two of our shallow-water fish, even if they were rays. The sawfish is a bactoid, more of a ray than a shark. Even though it has a long sharklike body, the gill slits lie on the undersides, whereas sharks have them on the sides. But since they appeared to be a mated pair, Nixon Griffis was consoled with the idea that we might have the first live birth of a sawfish in captivity. That gave him the prospect for the impossible that he so loved. Up to twenty-three sawfish have been born alive from a fifteen-foot female in the wild.

We kept them for a good two weeks before I finally got around to shipping them. I needed that much time to acclimate them properly, to induce them to eat in captivity, and to make sure they were in prime condition. But the truth was that I had grown fond of these great lumbering beasts with their long tooth-studded saws protruding from their sandpaper-skin brown bodies. Word got out, and people came from all over the area to see them. If ever there were monsters in the sea they were manifest in these raylike creatures.

They had their own personality. Nothing bothered them inside their new competitive and crowded environment. We had rock bass, grunts, sea catfish, and sea turtles snapping down food as quickly as we dropped it in. The slow-moving sawfish had a hard time competing during the feeding frenzies. But they compensated by swimming in the midst of the fish, slashing their saws from side to side, and causing all others to flee. Watching them, I had the feeling that the saw was far more than a mere weapon for bludgeoning. It was an extremely sensitive sensory organ. Just the touch of a herring or piece of fish with the tip of the bill makes the sawfish jump into action. It leaps forward and engulfs its meal in one or two gulps. Then, with full stomach, the sawfish sways back and forth and roots out the gravel, making a comfortable nest in the bottom.

We stopped feeding them two days before shipping so that they would travel on empty guts. The truth was that we had never shipped sawfish before, and I was nervous about it. A lot of money and effort were tied up in those two fish. It was a risk and a big challenge.

There was only one direct flight from Tallahassee to New York, with a stopover in Atlanta. The trouble was that it left at seven in the morning. We had to start packing at four.

The blaring alarm clock shattered my sleep, and I groped for it to avoid waking Anne. My collectors were coming in to pack at five. I had the coffee going, but barely had my eyes open. I was still in a deep fog, the kind in which you don't want to do anything. It was pitch-dark out and cold. The lights of my neighbors who go fishing at dawn had come on. Stars shone down in their lonely darkness. It was four-thirty, and it seemed more than enough time to go down, pack two sawfish, and have them at the airport by eight. I was beginning to feel better about the situation after coffee and with eyes open.

I had planned the packing strategy with my helpers, Leon Crum and Edward Keith, days before. We had done a thorough job of building the shipping containers. All day long saws screamed as they sliced through new plywood; hammers rhythmically tapped away, nailing it against the framing. Styrofoam sheets were cut out and inserted for thermal insulation and cushioning. The giant heavy-duty plastic bags were inserted, filled with filtered seawater. All that was needed were two sawfish to go into them with their bills wrapped to prevent them from perforating the bags.

I walked up the street to the laboratory in the chilly November air. I met my helpers coming to work, Leon with his coffee mug in hand, awake and anxious, Edward silent as usual, wearing his Caterpillar cap, his bushy hair protruding from beneath it.

We flicked on the lights of the wet lab, making us squint in the sudden artificial glare. All the creatures in the tanks were moving about, the two ridley turtles immediately swam over expecting food, and fish rose up and looked expectant. The spiny lobsters were out prowling away from their rock ledges. It's called *crepuscular activity*, in the sea or in the aquarium, animals' moving about during dawn and dusk. During the day they are quiet, and in the middle of the night activity shuts down. But now they were in full swing.

Both sawfishes were on the move. Call it ESP or whatever, but they seemed to know something was up from the time we entered the building. Day after day they lay there sluggishly, hardly moving a few inches until it was time to feed. Perhaps it was the vibrations of dragging the shipping crates over to the tank, or the lights' being suddenly turned on after total darkness, but they were gliding over the bottom, swimming a good four inches above the gravel, cruising around the circumference of the tank.

Edward watched them. "They look nervous or something," he said, yawning, trying to get the sleep out of his eyes.

"I reckon they got a right to be," Leon said with his usual enthusiasm. "You ready?"

"Let's get the female first," I said, as the flat brown carpet of fish with its protruding toothy bill cruised toward us. "She's a little smaller. We can practice on her."

Edward plunged his arms into the tank, grabbed her by the tail, and tried to jerk the fish up. But she swung around with her bill to get him, as he jumped away. Leon then grabbed at her middle, but the power of that animal was incredible. She again twisted from side to side and wrenched herself loose.

I managed to get a slippery hold on one of the three dorsal fins, but she was already free. The great armored ray bolted around the tank in a fury, slammed into the opposite side, and came charging back. I tried to work up the courage to grab her again, but looking at that ominous tooth-studded weapon made me hesitate. Again the image of that monster on the boat off Madagascar flooded my memory.

The male cruised past us, and because the female was still in a wild frenzy we decided he'd be easier. "Here goes," cried Leon. His bare arms shot into the tank and caught it around the middle. "Catch the bill!" he cried, pulling backward with all his strength. "Catch the bill!"

We rushed over to help him. Edward and I grabbed the head, to prevent the bill from swinging back and forth, and wrestled it down. Cold water splashed up and cascaded over us. "Get the tail; get the tail!" Leon cried.

Edward released for a moment to step around him, the sawfish gave a mighty thrust. I felt it wrench out of my headlock, the thick sandpapery hide scraping and abrading my skin. "Let go!" Edward cried. "We've got him." A cold wet shock went through me, as the tail delivered a walloping slap to my face. Leon bellowed as the toothy rostrum struck him and splashed back into the tank. A second later it was back in the water, churning the tank, free again.

"God almighty damn," my wounded collector shouted. "He's ruined me." He held up his arm, showing a series of small holes trickling blood. "That varmit's a whole lot stronger than I thought he'd be."

"You all right?" I asked, ineptly getting to my feet, feeling the sting and bruise.

"Yeah," he muttered, glowering at the fleeing sawfish. The whole tank was in turmoil: fish were swimming frantically in all directions; sea turtles were paddling as fast as they could, going around and around the tank.

For a moment we stood by watching the sawfishes bolt to and fro, trying to collect our wits. I glanced at my watch: five-thirty, dawn was breaking. We should have had one in the box by now, ready to start the next one, and they were just as far from being caught as when we first came in. "Maybe we should postpone this until we figure out a better way to catch them."

"Yeah," agreed Edward, vexed. "Like drain the whole damn tank, and then get them out."

I considered it, but that would take all day. All the other fish in the tank would have to be moved.

"No," Leon said stubbornly, "he's done made me mad now. I'm going to get him into that box if it has to be in little pieces." I knew from long experience that it was useless to argue with him when he took something personally. We would have to try again.

"All right, but if we don't get one in the next try, we'll have to postpone. I should be booking the shipment right now. We're way off schedule."

The male came swimming past me. Gathering courage I pounced on him, and instead of trying to haul him out, I pressed him down with all my might. He squirmed and fanned his tail, sending gravel flying in every direction. At the same time, to my chagrin, he was rubbing his soft yellow underbelly down into the gravel. I didn't want to hurt him, which is easy to do by causing internal hemorrhaging, but I didn't want him to hurt me either. "I've got him; I've got him; come on, grab him quick!"

Edward had a firm grip on his head and saw, I had his middle, and Leon gripped the tail. In one mighty heave we hoisted the 150-pound fish out of the water, and with grunts and gritted teeth, wrestled it down to the concrete floor and jumped back.

The sawfish went wild, gyrating back and forth, swinging its saw. "Throw water on the floor," I yelled, "or he'll scratch his belly."

Seawater cascaded down on the concrete floor from our five-gallon buckets until the sawfish was practically swimming again. Now there was nothing to do but stand back and let it fight itself out. After a good five minutes it began to weaken, the flurry of activity stopped, and again we tackled him. Only this time, in the world of air, we had the advantage.

While I sat on its back, knees pressing the ground to take my weight off, my helpers wound the bolt of cheesecloth around its bill, filling in the spaces between each of its twenty-two pairs of teeth, covering the sharp points until the entire saw was rendered harmless.

All during the bandaging, the big creature let out loud snorts, its gills opened and closed, and occasionally it gave a feeble wave of its fan tail. Its huge eyes seemed to be looking up at me with recrimination.

Nevertheless, we hoisted it into the waiting shipping crate, and I watched it lying in the oversize plastic bag while the oxygen was being jetted in. Once that majestic spiked nose caused terror to all at sea, and now it looked silly. We couldn't help laughing at the absurd sight of his huge bandaged nose.

The fish swatted his covered bill against the plastic, trying to shake it off, but the box was built so he could not turn around and had only enough room to move his saw slightly from side to side.

Leon took a deep breath and leaned up against the tank to rest. "I'll tell you one thing. I pity the poor SOB who has to unpack him on the other end."

Panting, tired, soaking wet, I looked at my watch and the numbers frightened me. "It's six-twenty!" I cried. "We've got to get the other one packed up in thirty minutes or we'll miss the plane. Maybe we should just ship this one."

"No, we can get 'em," said Edward. "I think I know how to do it this time."

He climbed up on top of the tank, then jumped into the water, wading rapidly across the tank holding a dip net. Without choice, we all jumped in and followed him, charged with adrenaline like soldiers going into battle. We waded over the gravel bottom, pushing sea turtles out of the way, rock bass, catfish, and sheepshead fleeing before us.

We knew this was dangerous because we were on the sawfish's turf. First it ran. Then, when cornered by our big stomping feet, it turned to fight. Edward's dip net snagged the approaching teeth, and before the fish could wrench it loose from his grasp, we dove down on top, pressing the female to the bottom, getting our arms beneath her, our hands on the bill. The smaller female managed to get in a few good slaps with her tail, and a few jabs at our hands with her teeth, but within the allotted time we were proficiently bandaging up her two-and-a-half-foot bill.

"You know," Leon panted, "we're getting better at this. Too bad there aren't any more sawfish to practice on."

Cold, drenched, and sore from our wounds, we hoisted each box into a separate pickup truck and sped off for the airport. I managed to call ahead, and they were waiting for our last-minute arrival.

Sawfish are sold by the foot. But it was never possible to get an exact measurement. Once or twice we tried putting a yardstick on the bottom of the tank. When they pounced on a piece of fish, and stopped to gobble it, we figured that the male was seven feet and the female about six-and-a-half. We planned to get an exact measurement when they were removed from the tank but ran out of time.

However, John Clark, the curator of the New York Aquarium, disagreed with our measurements. Not that he bothered to measure them either, when the staff unpacked the fish. He was chagrined. "Good Lord, did they have to wrap them up like Christmas presents?"

The entire staff of the aquarium, clerical help and visitors alike, clustered around to watch the curator trying to unpack the monsters, snipping the cheesecloth away from their bills.

At last they slid them into their largest tank and watched as the sawfish descended to the bottom, swimming around discovering the new and larger parameters of their confinement. Then they settled to the bottom and sat there opening and closing their gills. Within a day they were feeding.

The time had come to pay our bill, and John decided to settle the measurement dispute. He put on his wet suit and scuba tank and slid over the side, tape measure in hand, and approached the larger male.

Suddenly to his surprise he was under attack: the vorpal sword went snicker-snack! He was in a nightmare of teeth, coming at him from all directions, violently lunging. He bolted from the tank and scrambled out with the sawfish charging from the rear. The female was right behind him.

After that experience, we easily settled on a compromise price. For ten years when I periodically went up to New York, I sat beside the tank, watching my sawfishes with no little pride as the crowds pressed past. Of all the people staring at them, I felt uniquely blessed to see more than a strange-looking fish in an artificial environment.

The story had a sad ending. The mated pair lived together for seven years in the same tank, until a new curator took over. He was going to change things. The sawfish were dull, lumpish things, he declared, that always sat on the bottom—not a good exhibit. He demanded that they be separated. The male died almost immediately; the female perished several months later, some said, of a broken heart.

QUESTIONS FOR CRITICAL THINKING AND WRITING

1. There are two separate stories in this selection. Why might Rudloe have chosen to open with the story of spreading the ashes, and how does that story introduce the second sawfish story?

2. In your opinion, what does the sawfish represent in Rudloe's story? Select a scene that illustrates this representation and use it to support your statement.

3. Knowing that Rudloe is a conservationist and an environmental activist, is there anything in the narrative about his character that surprises you? How, in general, does knowing about an author before you read a text influence your reading?

DAMON RUNYON

Damon Runyon (1880–1946) was an American writer whose short stories centered on Broadway in New York City during Prohibition. His short stories "The Idyll of Miss Sarah Brown" and "Blood Pressure" were adapted into the well-known Broadway musical *Guys and Dolls*. In addition, he had a newspaper column called "The Brighter Side," which is where "The Stone Crab" originally appeared. Runyon died of throat cancer in 1946, and there is now a nonprofit cancer research foundation in his name, which grants millions of dollars each year to young scientists pursuing innovative cancer research.

Courtesy of Bettmann/Corbis.

BEFORE YOU READ

"The Stone Crab" is a short, humorous article about a Floridian delicacy and the tourists who are threatening to destroy it. Does your hometown or state have a delicacy like this that would be ruined if outsiders discovered it?

The Stone Crab 1930s

One of the more regrettable circumstances attendant upon the tourist invasion of Dade County, Florida, of recent Winters, was the discovery by visitors of the stone crab.

The home folks down in Dade County, Florida, have long esteemed the stone crab the greatest of native delicacies and can remember when they were so numerous that a man could dip a foot anywhere in Biscayne Bay and come up with a stone crab hanging on each toe. Or lacking the energy to dunk a pedal he could buy more stone crabs for a few bits than a horse could lug.

Since the Winter visitors got on to the stone crab, however, the crustaceans have become scarce and costly. They now sell by the karat. They are so expensive that the home folks are inclined to leave them on their menus. The visitors eat more of the stone crab nowadays and this is all the more deplorable when you reflect that stone crabs are really too good for visitors. A certificate of at least four years residence in Dade County should be required of every person desiring stone crabs.

The stone crab is an ornery looking critter that hangs out around the Florida Keys and nowhere else in the world. It is a sucker for a trap baited with fish. It bears some resemblance to the California crab, but is cooked and served differently and the taste is also different. Occasionally a Californian from up around San Francisco drifts into Dade County, Florida, and goes against stone crabs and right away he wants to go out in the kitchen and start an argument with the chef on the basis that the California cracked crab tastes better.

This is where we would not care to take sides. We always bear in mind the experience of a New York fellow who stepped between a Californian and a New Yorker who were arguing the respective merits of the California cracked crab and the Florida stone crab. The poor soul incautiously ventured the statement that the northern crab tastes better than either and he got slugged from two directions.

The stone crab is much larger than the northern crab and has a shell harder than a landlord's heart. In places in Dade County where stone crabs are served, the shell is cracked with a large wooden mallet before being set before the customer. Only the huge claws of the stone crab contain the edible meat. The body is waste, but when the live crab is weighed the body is included in the total poundage and the buyer pays by the pound.

The stone crab is cooked by boiling. A lot of people have tried to think up better ways, but boiling is best. It is served cold with hot melted butter with a dash of lemon in it on the side. Probably the right place in which to eat stone crabs would be the bathtub. The fingers are used in toying with them. Some high-toned folks use those little dinky oyster forks, but the fingers are far speedier and more efficient.

In Dade County prior to 1920, no one bothered much with stone crabs as an article of diet. Then the late Jim Allison, of Indianapolis, one of the builders of Miami Beach, who had an aquarium on the shores of Biscayne Bay loaded with aquatic fauna of various kinds, imported a Harvard professor to study and classify the local fish and one day this professor saw some boys with a bunch of stone crabs.

He wanted to know what they were going to do with them, and they said they were going to throw them away. The professor said that was bad judgement as the crabs were good eating, and somebody tried them and found he was right as rain. Biscayne Bay was full of stone crabs at that time, but harbor blasting and dredging chased them away and the great crabbing grounds are now to the south of Dade County, along the Keys, a Key being just a small island.

There is a restaurant at the south of Miami Beach known as Joe's which specializes in stone crabs. Joe's, the oldest and most famous restaurant on the beach, is conducted by Joe Weiss, whose father established the place around 1919. Weiss has his own boats operating during the stone crab season which runs from October 15 to May 15 and this gives him a big edge over the other restaurant men on the crabs. He uses as high as a thousand pounds of crabs a day.

The stone crab of Dade County seems to be the morro crab of Cuba with a Spanish accent. They are both ugly enough to enjoy some kinship. It is the look of the stone crab that has deterred many a Winter visitor to Dade County from eating it — many, but not enough to suit those of us who view the inroads of the visitors on the crab supply with genuine alarm.

QUESTIONS FOR CRITICAL THINKING AND WRITING

1. Runyon uses hyperbole and satire to establish a humorous tone in his article. Identify a few instances where he uses these elements for the sake of humor.

2. What is the purpose of the anecdote regarding the Californian arguing that the crab on the West Coast is better? How does Runyon feel about outsiders arguing that stone crabs are not as good as their regional crabs?

3. Do natives of a region have a greater claim on their surroundings and natural resources than visitors, especially in a place like Florida, where tourism is an essential aspect of the economy? Why or why not?

WALLACE STEVENS

Wallace Stevens (1875–1955) was an American poet from Pennsylvania. He took a circuitous route to poetry, first pursuing a career in law and then moving on to work as an executive at an insurance company. He wrote poetry on the side, and in 1955 won the Pulitzer Prize for *Collected Poems*. Helen Vendler in the *New York Times Book Review* said of Stevens: "[He] wished passionately to be above all a poet of twentieth-century America and its American English; and he had the luck . . . to write with increasing genius to the end of his life."

Courtesy of Bettmann/Corbis.

BEFORE YOU READ

If you have a difficult time understanding "The Idea of Order at Key West," you are not alone. Rather than viewing this as a negative, though, you can take ownership of your analysis of the poem. What do you think the poem means, and what makes the poem open to interpretation?

The Idea of Order at Key West   *1954*

She sang beyond the genius of the sea.
The water never formed to mind or voice,
Like a body wholly body, fluttering
Its empty sleeves; and yet its mimic motion
Made constant cry, caused constantly a cry,   5
That was not ours although we understood,
Inhuman, of the veritable ocean.

The sea was not a mask. No more was she.
The song and water were not medleyed sound
Even if what she sang was what she heard,   10
Since what she sang was uttered word by word.
It may be that in all her phrases stirred
The grinding water and the gasping wind;
But it was she and not the sea we heard.

For she was the maker of the song she sang.   15
The ever-hooded, tragic gestured sea
Was merely a place by which she walked to sing.
Whose spirit is this? we said, because we knew
It was the spirit that we sought and knew
That we should ask this often as she sang.   20

If it was only the dark voice of the sea
That rose, or even colored by many waves;
If it was only the outer voice of sky
And cloud, of the sunken coral water-walled,
However clear, it would have been deep air,   25
The heaving speech of air, a summer sound
Repeated in a summer without end
And sound alone. But it was more than that,
More even than her voice, and ours, among
The meaningless plungings of water and the wind,   30
Theatrical distances, bronze shadows heaped
On high horizons, mountainous atmospheres
Of sky and sea.

It was her voice that made
The sky acutest at its vanishing.   35
She measured to the hour its solitude.
She was the single artificer of the world
In which she sang. And when she sang, the sea
Whatever self it had, became the self
That was her song, for she was the maker. Then we,   40
As we beheld her striding there alone,
Knew that there never was a world for her
Except the one she sang and, singing, made.

Ramon Fernandez, tell me, if you know,
Why, when the singing ended and we turned   45
Toward the town, tell why the glassy lights,
The lights in the fishing boats at anchor there,
As the night descended, tilting in the air,
Mastered the night and portioned out the sea,
Fixing emblazoned zones and fiery poles,   50
Arranging, deepening, enchanting night.

Oh! Blessed rage for order, pale Ramon,
The maker's rage to order words of the sea,
Words of the fragrant portals, dimly-starred,
And of ourselves and of our origins,   55
In ghostlier demarcations, keener sounds.

QUESTIONS FOR CRITICAL THINKING AND WRITING

1. Stevens uses the pronouns *she* and *her* throughout the poem. What are these pronouns referring to? What or who is the subject of the poem?
2. In the final stanza, Stevens refers to "the maker's rage to order words of the sea." What do you think Stevens is describing here?
3. Stanza by stanza, Wallace's descriptions of the sea evolve. Assign a tone or an emotion to each stanza, and explain why you believe the stanza represents that emotion.

WALLACE STEVENS

A biographical note for Wallace Stevens appears on page 125.

BEFORE YOU READ

"O Florida, Venereal Soil" is Wallace Stevens's response to Florida. As you read, note what Stevens decides to include about the state. What are his overall feelings about the place, and how does he express them?

O Florida, Venereal Soil   *1922*

A few things for themselves,
Convolvulus and coral,
Buzzards and live-moss,
Tiestas from the keys,
A few things for themselves,   5
Florida, venereal soil,
(Disclose to the lover.)

The dreadful sundry of this world,
The Cuban, Polodowsky,
The Mexican women,   10
The negro undertaker
Killing the time between corpses
Fishing for crayfish . . .
Virgin of boorish births,

Swiftly in the nights,   15
In the porches of Key West,
Behind the bougainvilleas,
After the guitar is asleep,
Lasciviously as the wind,
You come tormenting,   20
Insatiable,

When you might sit,
A scholar of darkness,
Sequestered over the sea,
Wearing a clear tiara   25
Of red and blue and red,
Sparkling, solitary, still,
In the high sea-shadow.

Donna, donna, dark,
(Stooping in indigo gown)   30
And cloudy constellations,
Conceal yourself or disclose
Fewest things to the lover—
A hand that bears a thick-leaved fruit,
A pungent bloom against your shade.   35

QUESTIONS FOR CRITICAL THINKING AND WRITING

1. The word *Venereal* is used here as a reference to Venus, the Roman goddess of love. What other specifically female allusions or imagery appear in the poem?
2. What is Stevens referring to in the second stanza with the line "The dreadful sundry of this world"?
3. What do the last two lines of the poem evoke? How is the language in those last two lines different from the language in the rest of the poem?

HARRIET BEECHER STOWE

Harriet Beecher Stow (1811–1896) is best known for her novel *Uncle Tom's Cabin*, but she was a prolific writer in her lifetime, publishing more than thirty books. She was born in Connecticut and was the sixth child of eleven siblings. She began wintering in Florida after the Civil War, both for the mild weather—as the following essay illustrates—and to work for racial equality. Stowe's brother, Charles Beecher, had opened a school for emancipated slaves, which Harriet and her husband helped with. She spent winters in Florida for almost fifteen years, before her husband's failing health prevented them from making the trip south.

BEFORE YOU READ

Harriet Beecher Stowe warns that visitors to Florida should not "hope for too much." As you read, pay close attention to both the positive and negative attributes of the state that Stowe describes. Does she portray the state fairly, and why might she warn those who want to visit?

The Wrong Side of the Tapestry 1873

It is not to be denied that full half of the tourists and travellers that come to Florida return intensely disappointed, and even disgusted. Why? Evidently because Florida, like a piece of embroidery, has two sides to it — one side all tag-rag and thrums, without order or position; and the other side showing flowers and arabesques and brilliant coloring. Both these sides exist. Both are undeniable, undisputed facts, not only in the case of Florida, but of every place and thing under the sun. There is a right side and a wrong side to every thing.

Now, tourists and travellers generally come with their heads full of certain romantic ideas of waving palms, orange-groves, flowers, and fruit, all bursting forth in tropical abundance; and, in consequence, they go through Florida with disappointment at every step. If the banks of the St. John's were covered with orange-groves, if they blossomed every month in the year, if they were always loaded with fruit, if pineapples and bananas grew wild, if the flowers hung in festoons from tree to tree, if the ground were enamelled with them all winter long, so that you saw nothing else, then they would begin to be satisfied.

But, in point of fact, they find, in approaching Florida, a dead sandy level, with patches behind them of rough coarse grass, and tall pine-trees, whose tops are so far in the air that they seem to cast no shade, and a little scrubby underbrush. The few houses to be seen along the railroad are the forlornest of huts. The cattle that stray about are thin and poverty-stricken, and look as if they were in the last tottering stages of starvation.

Then, again, winter, in a semi-tropical region, has a peculiar desolate untidiness, from the fact that there is none of that clearing of the trees and shrubs which the sharp frosts of the northern regions occasion. Here the leaves, many of them, though they have lost their beauty, spent their strength, and run their course, do not fall thoroughly and cleanly, but hang on in ragged patches, waiting to be pushed off by the swelling buds of next year. In New England, Nature is an up-and-down, smart, decisive house-mother, that has her times and seasons, and brings up her ends of life with a positive jerk. She will have no shilly-shally. When her time comes, she clears off the gardens and forests thoroughly and once for all, and they are clean. Then she freezes the ground solid as iron; and then she covers all up with a nice pure winding-sheet of snow, and seals matters up as a good housewife does her jelly tumblers under white-paper covers. There you are fast and cleanly. If you have not got ready for it, so much the worse for you! If your tender roots are not taken up, your cellar banked, your doors listed, she can't help it: it's your own lookout, not hers.

But Nature down here is an easy, demoralized, indulgent old grandmother, who has no particular time for anything, and does everything when she happens to feel like it. "Is it winter, or isn't it?" is the question that is likely often to occur in the settling month of December, when everybody up North has put away summer clothes, and put all their establishments under winter-orders.

Consequently, on arriving in mid-winter time the first thing that strikes the eye is the ragged, untidy look of the foliage and shrubbery. About one-third of the trees are deciduous, and stand entirely bare of leaves. The rest are evergreen, which by this time, having come through the fierce heats of summer, have acquired a seared and dusky hue, different from the vivid brightness of early

You throw snowballs for me while I pick oranges for you, 1947. Postcards like these, both modern versions and retro-updates with the same look, are still popular today.
Courtesy of the State Archives of Florida.

spring. In the garden you see all the half-and-half proceedings which mark the indefinite boundaries of the season. The rosebushes have lost about half their green leaves. Some varieties, however, in this climate, seem to be partly ever-green. The La Marque and the crimson rose, sometimes called Louis Philippe, seem to keep their last year's foliage till spring pushes it off with new leaves.

Once in a while, however, Nature, like a grandmother in a fret, comes down on you with a most unexpected snub. You have a cold spell — an actual frost. During the five years in which we have made this our winter residence, there have twice been frosts severe enough to spoil the orange-crop, though not materially injuring the trees.

This present winter has been generally a colder one than usual; but there have been no hurtful frosts. But one great cause of disgust and provocation of tourists in Florida is the occurrence of these "cold snaps." It is really amusing to see how people accustomed to the tight freezes, the drifting snow wreaths, the stinging rain, hail, and snow, of the Northern winter, will *take on* when the thermometer goes down to 30° or 32°, and a white frost is seen out of doors. They are perfectly outraged. "*Such* weather! If this is your Florida winter, deliver me!" All the while they could walk out any day into the woods, as we have done, and gather eight or ten varieties of flowers blooming in the open air, and eat radishes and lettuce and peas grown in the garden.

Well, it is to be confessed that the cold of warm climates always has a peculiarly aggravating effect on the mind. A warm region is just like some people who get such a character for good temper, that they never can indulge themselves even in an earnest disclaimer without everybody crying out upon them, "What puts you in such a passion?" and so forth. So Nature, if she generally sets up for amiability during the winter months, cannot be allowed a little tiff now and then, a white frost, a cold rain-storm, without being considered a monster.

It is to be confessed that the chill of warm climates, when they are chilly, is peculiar; and travellers should prepare for it, not only in mind, but in wardrobe, by carrying a plenty of warm clothing, and, above all, an inestimable India-rubber bottle, which they can fill with hot water to dissipate the chill at night. An experience of four winters leads us to keep on about the usual winter clothing until March or April. The first day after our arrival, to be sure, we put away all our furs as things of the past; but we keep abundance of warm shawls, and, above all, wear the usual flannels till late in the spring.

Invalids seeking a home here should be particularly careful to secure rooms in which there can be a fire. It is quite as necessary as at the North; and, with this comfort, the cold spells, few in number as they are, can be easily passed by.

Our great feature in the Northern landscape, which one never fails to miss and regret here, is the grass. The *nakedness* of the land is an expression that often comes over one. The peculiar sandy soil is very difficult to arrange in any tidy fashion. You cannot make beds or alleys of it: it all runs together like a place where hens have been scratching; and consequently it is the most difficult thing in the world to have ornamental grounds.

At the North, the process of making a new place appear neat and inviting is very rapid. One season of grass-seed, and the thing is done. Here, however, it is the most difficult thing in the world to get turf of any sort to growing. The Bermuda grass, and a certain coarse, broad-leafed turf, are the only kind that can stand the summer heat; and these never have the beauty of well-ordered Northern grass.

Now, we have spent anxious hours and much labor over a little plot in our back-yard, which we seeded with white clover, and which, for a time, was green and lovely to behold; but, alas! the Scripture was too strikingly verified: "When the sun shineth on it with a burning heat, it withereth the grass, and the grace of the fashion of it perisheth."

The fact is that people cannot come to heartily like Florida till they *accept* certain deficiencies as the necessary shadow to certain excellences. If you want to live in an orange-orchard, you must give up wanting to live surrounded by green grass. When we get to the new heaven and the new earth, then we shall have it all right. There we shall have a climate at once cool and bracing, yet hot enough to mature oranges and pineapples. Our trees of life shall bear twelve manner of fruit, and yield a new one every month. Out of juicy meadows green as emerald, enamelled with every kind of flower, shall grow our golden orange-trees, blossoming and fruiting together as now they do. There shall be no mosquitoes, or gnats, or black-flies, or snakes; and, best of all, there shall be no fretful people. Everybody shall be like a well-tuned instrument, all sounding in accord, and never a semitone out of the way.

Meanwhile, we caution everybody coming to Florida: Don't hope for too much. Because you hear that roses and callas blossom in the open air all winter, and flowers abound in the woods, don't expect to find an eternal summer. Prepare yourself to see a great deal that looks rough and desolate and coarse; prepare yourself for some chilly days and nights; and, whatever else you neglect

The Stowe family on the porch of their house in Mandarin, where they wintered from 1867 until 1882.
State of Florida Archives.

to bring with you, bring the resolution, strong and solid, always to make the best of things.

For ourselves, we are getting reconciled to a sort of tumble-down, wild, picnicky kind of life — this general happy-go-luckiness which Florida inculcates. If we painted her, we should not represent her as a neat, trim damsel, with starched linen cuffs and collar: she would be a brunette, dark but comely, with gorgeous tissues, a general disarray and dazzle, and with a sort of jolly untidiness, free, easy, and joyous.

The great charm, after all, of this life, is its outdoorness. To be able to spend your winter out of doors, even though some days be cold; to be able to sit with windows open; to hear birds daily; to eat fruit from trees, and pick flowers from hedges, all winter long—is about the whole of the story. This you can do; and this is why Florida is life and health to the invalid.

We get every year quantities of letters from persons of small fortunes, asking our advice whether they had better move to Florida. For our part, we never advise people to *move* anywhere. As a general rule, it is the person who feels the inconveniences of a present position, so as to want to move, who will feel the inconvenience of a future one. Florida has a lovely winter; but it has also three formidable summer months, July, August, and September, when the heat is excessive, and the liabilities of new settlers to sickness so great, that we should never wish to take the responsibility of bringing anybody here. It is true that a very comfortable number of people do live through them; but still it is not a joke, by any means, to move to a new country. The first colony in New England lost just half its members in the first six months. The rich bottom-lands around Cincinnati proved graves to many a family before they were brought under cultivation.

But Florida is peculiarly adapted to the needs of people who can afford two houses, and want a refuge from the drain the winter makes on the health. As people now have summer-houses at Nahant or Rye, so they might, at a small expense, have winter-houses in Florida, and come here and be at home. That is the great charm—to be at home. A house here can be simple and inexpensive, and yet very charming. Already, around us a pretty group of winter-houses is rising: and we look forward to the time when there shall be many more; when, all along the shore of the St. John's, cottages and villas shall look out from the green trees.

QUESTIONS FOR CRITICAL THINKING AND WRITING

1. Many of the essays in this book show the state of Florida as a dichotomy. How does Stowe do this, and what conclusions does she draw about the state in terms of the different sides of Florida?

2. What advice does Stowe give to those who ask if they should move to Florida? How does this advice reflect her overall vision of the region?

3. How does Stowe describe the "cold" in Florida, and why is it "peculiarly aggravating"?

DIEGO VICENTE TEJERA

Diego Vicente Tejera (1848–1903) was a Cuban poet and short story writer in addition to being a political activist. He traveled around the world, living in New York, Venezuela, Barcelona, and Key West. Upon his return to Cuba, he founded the Cuban Socialist Party and the Labor Party in 1901. He was a skilled orator and often gave speeches like "Education in Democratic Societies."

Courtesy of Biblioteca Nacional de Cuba
José Martí.

BEFORE YOU READ

"Education in Democratic Societies" was a speech Tejera gave at the San Carlos Institute in Key West, Florida, in 1887. As you read, keep in mind the intended audience of the speech. How might the audience have influenced Tejera's choices in terms of language, tone, and subject matter?

From *Education in Democratic Societies*   *1887*

TRANSLATED BY CAROLINA HOSPITAL

The course that I want to follow for these humble conferences demands that I consider today the type of education provided in our society in order to see if it is appropriate for a new democratic people . . . for a people without traditions, a people unconcerned, a bit frivolous, a bit vain, a bit finicky, with a vivid imagination and strong passions; but with a natural kindness and a clear intelligence.

It is a delicate topic which should be studied by all our scholars. I will only be able to scratch the surface, but we should begin to call attention to this topic so that as we reshape other aspects of our culture, we also consider education in a new way.

Indeed, it would not be a waste of time to speak a bit, first, about what education unfortunately means to the popular classes and what it should mean instead. Indeed, education establishes differences between individuals, differences which can injure those who feel inferior even though these differences may be purely social and to a certain extent legitimate. If education were what it should be morally, social differences would hardly be noticeable and would not be so shameful for anyone. If education would in truth improve individuals, then its first effect would be to make people kinder, and disinclined to demonstrate superiority in their treatment of those who had not been educated to the same extent. True education would even out the rough edges in people's characters, and leave only smooth polished surfaces, so that in forced daily social dealings there would not be scrapes nor conflicts, but rather peaceful encounters. Given that, I would not hesitate in calling anyone—even if such a person had university degrees, wore elegant suits, and were full of delicacies and politeness in social gatherings—a spoiled brat, if this person behaved with snobbery and superiority in the presence of another whom they considered inferior.

Unfortunately, individuals such as these, of both genders, abound in our society, and that is the first reason I have for suspecting that our education is bad. They abound, I say, and we can blame them for the negative attitudes the popular classes have against the so-called cultured ones. These ignorant people are making education disagreeable, by giving it unheard-of airs; proof that they confuse—the most awkward ones—dignity with haughtiness and natural advancement with phony loftiness. They don't realize that from the moment they commit their first vulgarity, just one, they deserve the name of vulgarian, which means uneducated. And they fall, as a matter of fact, to a lower level than those they wish to scorn. . . .

Good moral and intellectual education are not only desirable, but necessary in democratic societies. The direction and government of our things must be entrusted to all, and if the responsibility were to rest more on one class than another, it would be on the working class. Because of its numbers, it would have more weight on the general decisions.

But education for public life must rest on private education, which begins with the parents before the infant even opens its eyes: the citizen must leave the home already formed. And it is here, before the spectacle I witness in our future free homeland, where suddenly I see our present education with all its deformity and deficiency. The brutal Spanish regime, to which we have been subjected, has not prepared us, has not been able to prepare us for the exercise of freedom and human rights, nor has it allowed us to acquire great domestic virtues. By distancing us from business affairs, it has made us become indifferent to them. Furthermore, they have corrupted our customs with their example of immorality always triumphant, thus obscuring the clarity of our principles; and I haven't spoken of how they have purposely and maliciously perverted us, creating and fostering vices which we will carry with us for a long time.

Thus, we have to proceed, without any delay, with implementing the total education of the individual as well as the citizen. Because it is impossible, from every which way, given our inclinations and limitations, to enter our new life without stirring it up, perhaps forever. We are still *colonos* in character, and if we do not transform ourselves, we risk the danger of not knowing what else to do except repeat the dreadful pattern of the old colony. . . .

In any case, we should begin to fulfill the new responsibilities imposed by our new circumstances, instilling as soon as possible in our families the principles of a rational education to substitute the insincere education received during colonial times.

Was it insincere, yes? Didn't they educate us only for private life? Was it not the attitude that the ultimate purpose of education was to shine in social gatherings? The poor instruction we were given, was it not generally classic and for adornment? Didn't we maintain a rancid preoccupation with caste, affirming that in society two types of individuals exist, those that are our equal and those that are inferior, and the first should be treated with consideration and the latter with disdain, so as to keep them at a distance? Was it not repeated time after time that work in itself was denigrating, acceptable only of necessity and, given this, that careers providing benefits and fame should be chosen, and manual rugged occupations should be left for the lower classes? Were we not taught to spend money on objects of vanity and to put on airs, whether we were rich or not? Was it not considered in good favor to drink, play, engage in duels, dress well without paying the tailor, and publicly and verbally dishonor women? Was disgusting gossip and idle chatter not promoted in every home, these vices which have turned our society, which is at heart good and generous, into a seething commotion of ill-will? Did we not talk about the pillages of the bandit in the countryside and the robberies of the government employee and the commercial smuggler in the city as witty accomplishments? Was it not general practice to mock the laws, and especially to violate, *de guapo*, police mandates? . . .

Well, now, we should do exactly the opposite; we have to educate ourselves for a serious and honorable social life and for a public life raised against difficulties and dangers; we should educate ourselves not to be dandies at social gatherings, but rather men on whose actions depend the success or failure of their country. We should be educated to respect all our citizens, treating them all with equal consideration, and treating with even greater consideration those who are weaker and less fortunate. We should be educated in work, seeing it as a blessing, not only because it develops the national wealth, but because it allows the children of the popular classes to reach, in a safe and decorous way, the level of classes privileged in other ways. We should be educated in an austere economy that creates fortunes and is proof of morality in the one who practices it; it will allow us, with the fruit of our labor, all the legitimate satisfactions accorded, while absolutely shunning those of mere vanity, the most costly and impure, the most unworthy of a true democracy. We should be educated in studies, providing nourishment for the spirit, redeeming us from the slavery of ignorance and furnishing us with the rewards that science and art can offer us. We should be educated in the exercise of strict virtues that ennoble and preserve a republic, rejecting vice, as appealing as it may seem, censuring those that are irresponsible, as well as those that offend women. We should be educated in charity and goodwill, eliminating in the home the first sign of ill-will or neighborhood gossip that may creep in, because respect for others is the best safeguard to self-respect and because the pleasure of insulting others can lead to gratuitous injury, the pleasure of the wicked, which would reveal the end of kindness in our society. We should be educated to defend the needs of the community in which we live, considering our enemies those who steal whether in the countryside or in the city. We should be educated in a profound respect for the law and the precepts of our community, which are the expression of our will and without which a society cannot endure. We should learn that fortunes are acquired only through our own intelligence and effort, abandoning gambling, a practice which takes more than gives and which destroys the entire point of education, which is to dignify and enrich, while this vice impoverishes and degrades. In sum, we should be educated to look at ourselves and others scrupulously, to keep our cities, our homes, and ourselves physically and morally clean, and to shun anything that might contaminate the body or poison the soul. . . .

No man should enter social life without possessing the sum of knowledge not only useful but necessary to think critically and independently. That sum of knowledge, those notions of natural and political science, of philosophy and history, could form a compulsory program of education in Cuba and would be the indispensable degree for entering the career of life. The classic degree, the old degree, was not appropriate, since it was a pedantic construct of inconsistent and foolish topics. . . .

I believe that our current education is detestable; I believe that a large part of our so-called cultured class should abandon unjustified pretensions to a distinguished origin and lose those false aristocratic airs, so unbecoming, thus assuming to the fullest the democratic spirit, which, by the way, does not exclude social distinction based on virtue, courteous behavior, and proper manners. I believe our culture should completely renovate its education, fixing defects belonging to its race and vices acquired under the terrible Spanish domination; I believe this moral education should be accompanied by intellectual education, providing now, as a free people, an intellectual level high enough to be able to practice with discretion political sovereignty and to prevent the rise of an oligarchy among us. You can see that the problem has a simple exposition, which leads us to assume its resolution can also be easy. I judge it so, and I expect the most from my people, who, in spite of their defects and vices, possess solid natural virtue. Foreigners are beginning to recognize them; already an important America admires the way the Cuban people have carried out their long immigration, struggling well in a disadvantageous environment, maintaining themselves with decorum because of their untiring labor, their temperate tastes, and the moderation of their customs, not contributing to the statistics of crime by foreigners in this vast country. Reason for pride and hope. These immigrants will take back to their homeland the habits acquired in this great school of democracy. . . .

QUESTIONS FOR CRITICAL THINKING AND WRITING

1. What does Tejera say education means to the popular classes, and what does he argue it should mean, conversely?
2. According to Tejera, how does the "current education" he discusses encourage an unequal class system, and how does he propose to change that?
3. What literary elements (i.e., repetition and assonance) does Tejera use to enhance his speech? Why might these elements make the speech more effective when spoken?

FRED J. WELLS

Not much is known about the author of this 1895 piece, which also appears in a collection of nineteenth- and early twentieth-century literature called *Tales of Old Florida*, edited by Frank Oppel and Tony Meisel.

BEFORE YOU READ

The fish featured in "An Adventure with a Tarpon" is a game fish and does not have desirable meat. Most tarpon fishermen catch and release, and the sport is more about the thrill of the hunt because the fish put up such a good fight. As you read Wells's essay, pay attention to the motivations behind the fishermen's actions. Why do they want to catch the tarpon, and what are they willing to do to get it?

An Adventure with a Tarpon   *1895*

Last October my friend Beatty came to me, to discuss plans for a fishing trip to the South. As anglers are wont to do, we discussed the advantages and disadvantages of many points, and at last decided in favor of Southern Alabama.

We went to Magnolia Springs on the Fish River. This river, as its name indicates, abounds in fish of various species. It is not very wide, averaging perhaps five hundred yards, but the water is deep and very clear. It flows into Mobile Bay about five miles below the Springs, and large fish, such as tarpon, gar, red-fish, crevalia, shark, etc., ascend the river to feed upon the plentiful smaller fry. We often saw large fish rise to the surface and make a dart through a school of mullets, scattering them in every direction and forcing some to leap several feet into the air. This drama of pursuers and pursued is one of the strange scenes characteristic of Southern waters. The porpoises were also great destroyers. On the mud flats near the mouth of the river, I have seen them rushing through the shallow water with mouths wide open, taking in everything that could not get out of the way.

The river flows through tracts of heavy timber and through broad marshes, its banks bearing live-oak, cypress, and Southern trees embracing more than one hundred varieties. At its mouth it is perhaps two hundred yards wide, with an average depth of from forty to fifty feet. The bottom is composed of fine, hard sand.

We had in our service a colored man, Louis Collins, one of the best guides in the South. He has lived on the banks of Fish River all his life, and is thoroughly acquainted with the habits and peculiarities of the different species of fish. The morning after our arrival we found him waiting for us with his flat-bottomed boat, made especially for fishing. He rowed us to the mouth of the river, and on the way down we trolled with phantom minnows, catching plenty of trout and red-fish, but failing to strike any larger fish. More than once during the day we were electrified by the sight of tarpon, or silver fish as the natives call them, leaping to their full length from the water and falling flat on their sides. The resounding splashes the great fellows made, the gleam of their silvery scales in the sunlight, and the mighty swirl they made as they went under, set our hearts a-thumping, but we were not fortunate enough to have one of them take our hook.

We caught red-fish, one of which weighed full thirty pounds, and made a fight for about forty-five minutes before he could be brought near enough to the boat to be harpooned; several sharks of the smaller species, weighing from twenty to forty pounds, and many smaller fish of different kinds. An exciting feature of this sport is that the tide brings the salt-water fish into the river, so that one seldom knows what kind of a fish he has hooked until it is brought to the surface.

The first fish I caught took the bait and went off with it as if he would never stop. I finally succeeded in turning him, and after about thirty minutes of lively work brought him within view only to find that I had hooked a shark. For several days we fished up and down the river with varied success, seeing many tarpon but not being able to hook one.

One morning we left the Springs about eight o'clock with the intention of spending the day at the mouth of the river. When about half way to the mouth we noticed a swell in the water caused by a large fish swimming slowly up stream near the surface. He was quite a distance away on our left and near the shore, which at that point was marshy and covered with cane brakes and cypress saplings. The guide turned the boat so that it would float in the direction of the fish, and after warning us to keep perfectly still he prepared his harpoon, or gig. The harpoon had a handle about ten feet long and was so arranged that the iron barbed tip would loosen from the handle. A large cord one hundred feet in length was fastened to the harpoon and was wound on a wooden float. After unwinding about twenty-five feet of line and shoving the boat a little more toward shore, the guide stood up ready for action.

The boat was now in such a position that if the fish did not change its course it would pass within a few feet of us. Up to this time the fish had been so deeply submerged that we could not determine his species, but when he was within about six rods of us he came up so near the surface that we could see the narrow elongation of the dorsal fin above the water.

"A silver fish," the guide whispered, and motioned to us not to move. There was a moment of tense excitement as we slowly and silently floated toward our intended victim. Would the fish continue to swim near the surface or would he disappear in the depths? Knowing that the guide was an expert with the harpoon, I felt confident that if we could once get within throwing distance some lively fun would result. Nearer we approached until the fish was nearly opposite and about fifteen feet away, and then suddenly the guide straightened himself up and raising the harpoon above his head, hurled it forward with practiced skill.

For an instant all was still, then the huge fish leaped his full length into the air and we could see that the iron had entered his side just back of the head. He came down with a tremendous splash, turned in a wild swirl of water, rushed head-on like lightning at us and jumped clean over the boat!

I was sitting in the bow and he passed over just in front of me. All that I saw was a silvery something going through the air like a cannon-ball. To say that I dodged would be expressing it mildly. I never came so near falling over backward from a boat, and failed, in my life. As for the guide, who was standing up, he simply dropped.

I had seen fish jump over a boat before, but I never expected to be made a target for a fish weighing over two hundred pounds and I never want to again. As he struck the water he went down out of sight, jerking the line out of the hands of the guide and taking line and float with him. The boat seemed to be going over, but we heard a crash of a broken board and it righted. The line had caught in a crack in the end of one of the short, bottom boards and had split the board about half way and then broken it in two at a large knot. The board being defective was all that saved us from taking a watery bath and in all probability losing the fish, if nothing worse.

After a few moments we saw the float come to the surface about twenty rods away, up the river, and we guessed that the line had unwound of itself. The fish had evidently found the bottom and was moving slowly. We rowed as fast as possible, caught the float, and then made for the shore. The fish came along without struggling very much, although pulling hard. As we neared the shore the guide seized the cord, jumped out into water up to his waist, and made for the bank. He commenced to pull the fish in, and had succeeded in getting about thirty feet of slack line, when the fish turned and went away fast. The guide, seeing he could not hold him, ran and took a half turn around a small cypress sapling about two inches in diameter, but the fish was going so fast and with such force that he bent the tree over, broke the limbs, jerked the line out of the guide's hands, and away he went up stream. The guide got into the boat and we chased the float again. The tarpon jumped out of the water several times, shaking his head as they do when hooked, but the harpoon was in too deep to be loosened. The struggle reminded me more of trying to break a wild mustang than of anything I know of.

We followed the float for fully a quarter of a mile before we overtook it. At last we secured it and rowed again to the shore. The guide jumped out in the marsh and just had time to pass the line around a small tree before the fish started off again. As the guide felt the line straighten out and saw the tree bend over, he noticed a root under which there was room to pass the float and he quickly took a half hitch around it, having just enough slack line to do so. The fish bent the sapling the same as he did the first one and straightened out the line. It was a question whether or not the line, which was a large cord, could stand the pull. All were now on shore and when finally the fish relaxed the strain we kept the line taut and carefully pulled it in. Twice the fish started off, but was quickly turned, it being evident that his strength was fast giving out. We at last hauled him to the bank and found we had a magnificent specimen of the tarpon. The harpoon had gone through the flesh into his vitals, and no doubt that was what sapped his strength, for he died in a very short time.

On measuring him we found he was six feet seven inches in length, with a spread of tail of eighteen inches. The mouth had an expanse of seven inches, and the diameter of the eye was two inches. The narrow extension of the dorsal fin, which we had first seen above the water, was eighteen inches long and about an inch wide. The scales measured as much as four inches in diameter the long way, and twelve inches in circumference. After examining the head and mouth I wondered that tarpon are ever killed with hook and line. The lower jaw is a solid bone, and the flesh, or muscle, is so hard that a hook should be easily shaken loose from it.

We put the fish across the boat near the stern, and pulled back to the Springs, feeling highly elated with our morning's work. The guide told us it was the largest silver fish caught in that section, and I have never heard of a larger one being taken anywhere. The people at Mobile expressed their astonishment at its size, and also at the fact that it was caught so far from the mouth of the river.

We did not have any means of weighing the fish, but it certainly weighed over two hundred pounds. I would have given a great deal for the privilege of taking him North just as he came from the water, but that was impossible. We arranged with a couple of colored men to take off the skin. This we preserved as best we could with arsenic, and succeeded in carrying it home, but as it could not be preserved we had to throw it away, after taking off the scales. The head was mounted, and now adorns the museum in our High School building.

QUESTIONS FOR CRITICAL THINKING AND WRITING

1. What role does the "colored" guide play in the story? Is he given his due recognition, or is his role minimized in the story?

2. It is common in essays about the natural world to have a passage in which the human is humbled by nature. Where in this essay does the natural world show its power?

3. After the fishermen caught the tarpon, what did they do with the dead fish? Keeping in mind that this essay was penned in 1895, would this still be considered acceptable? Why or why not?

4. **CONNECT TO ANOTHER READING.** Compare Jack Rudloe's "The Elusive Saw-fish" (p. III) and Fred J. Wells's "An Adventure with a Tarpon." What are the similarities in the story of the hunt, and what are the major differences? What does fishing represent to the respective authors?

RICK WILBER

Rick Wilber (b. 1948) is a journalism professor at the University of South Florida in Tampa. He has published numerous short story collections and a novel, *Rum Point*, which focuses on baseball — one of his most visited subjects. He has published more than fifty poems in magazines and journals, and he is an avid reader and writer of science fiction.

Courtesy of Rick Wilber.

BEFORE YOU READ

Wilber's short story "Finals" takes place in a dystopian future where everything bad has been exaggerated and life has become unlivable. Think of two or three essays you've read in this book that express similar ideas, but in a straightforward, journalistic manner. How are those ideas reflected in this story?

Finals   *1989*

> The sun was shining on the sea
>   Shining with all his might;
> He did his very best to make
>   The billows smooth and bright—
> And this was odd, because it was
>   The middle of the night.
>   — Lewis Carroll

I

Sean-Tomas Kyoshi Miller wants to go to university today, but it's been closed again. His European Finals are next week, and he's still a little shaky in conversational German, so he could use the lab time. He's OK, he figures, in Italian, French, and Spanish, and he's got the Contemporary Society part sussed all the way around. But the conversational German, for some reason, still has him worried. And if he doesn't pass that test. . . .

He doesn't want to think about that, about failing. His future rests on passing that test, so he can make probationary. Next year there'll be the Asian

Finals. Pass them and he's in full. But for now, he thinks, focus it in. First things first. Get that German down.

Still, he sighs, there's nothing he can do about it today. When university's closed, it's closed tight. Power outages, gunfights, bombs and bomb threats—it's always one of those, sometimes all three. It's a wonder he's managed to learn anything at all under the circumstances.

He is lying on his back in his too-small bed, staring vacantly at the ceiling. He notices the diagonal crack that has lengthened by another few inches in its march across the room. The ceiling needs to be fixed up, no doubt about that. The ceiling, the room, the house, the whole neighborhood, hell, the whole damn country—it all needs to be fixed up somehow.

Won't happen, though, he thinks. Just won't happen, no matter what Grandpa thinks. Instead it'll be the same slow slide, the long slow slide.

And Sean-Tomas wants out of it, at least as far out as he can get—out of Tampa and its slow death and its decay and its violence. He shakes his head to think of it, about how it's supposed to be better here than most places in the country. He shakes his head, takes a deep breath, tries to concentrate as he looks up at that cracked ceiling, and tries to recite his German verbs. These little verbs, after all, are his maglev route out of here, right into the Zone.

The Zone, that's what he wants. The Tourist Zone, where he'll have a chance to make something out of all this. That's what next week's, next year's, test is all about. Getting into the Zone.

There is a sudden banging on the door, it's Grandpa with that heavy cane he uses to take the weight off his arthritic left knee. And he hits the door hard, like he always does, announcing himself to his grandson, his favorite grandson, his only one, now, since Raffy was killed in the food riots four, no, five years ago.

"Sean-Tomas, what you doing lying here staring at that ceiling, boy? I thought you had a test coming up on Monday. Gonna get that Tourist Card, right? Gonna get out of here. Why aren't you off at that school?"

"Hi. Grandpa. I'm working on my German. The university's closed again and I can't get into the language lab, so I'm just doing what I can here."

He sits up, reaches over to the pressed wood desk that is falling apart already, despite how much it cost him and how proud he was to get it, and grabs the old German textbook.

He opens it at random, tries to pay attention to the verbs, figuring that's what Grandpa wants, that must be why he came banging into the room. Grandpa really wants him to get that card, get into the Zone.

But then the cane slaps down hard right onto the open spine of the book and Grandpa, gravelly-voiced but with that hint of gentleness that sneaks through so often, says, "You need a break, son. You been at that for weeks. You're ready. You know it."

Sean-Tomas smiles. "I know, Grandpa, I know. But I wanted to run through the conversational exercises one more time. It might help."

Grandpa looks at the boy—eighteen, put together right, could've played ball back in the old days. Got a fullback's body, thick but tight, with wide shoulders, trim waist, powerful calves and thighs. Could've played, been a Gator, maybe, like his Grandpa. Famous, maybe.

But no, no more of that nonsense. All that's long over with. And the boy looks tired, too. Been studying too damn much, worrying all the time about those Finals. Boy can use a day off.

"You come with me, Sean-Tomas," Grandpa says gruffly, putting his plan into action. "I got us a little excursion figured out. You're gonna like this, we're going into the Zone, see that sub-orbital come in with all them Japanese. It'll be good for you, show you what you got coming when you ace those Finals.

"C'mon, put some good clothes on and get yourself ready. I got us permits, ration cards to get us there and back on the 'rail, everything, even some spending money in Eurocoin."

Sean-Tomas looks up at his grandfather. He doesn't believe this, doesn't believe what he's hearing. Into the Zone? Ration cards? Permits? The new sub-orbital? What's got into Grandpa? Why's he doing this? How is he doing this? Sean-Tomas is speechless.

"It's true, boy. I got the permits, the cards, everything. Let's go."

They go.

II

The maglev 'rail runs on time. Everything for the tourists and the Wallys runs on time, works right, gets proper maintenance. The Euros expect it, and they get it or they won't come back. And now, with the sub-orbital, the Japanese will be here, too, and they're even crazier than the Euros about things working right, about things being, you know, tight, on-time. And then the Wallys, of course, the lucky few living behind the walled-in, safely suburban neighborhoods, they just benefit, reap the profits, from all this touristic perfection.

Grandpa's thinking all this as he and Sean-Tomas waltz coolly onto the 'rail at The Busch Gardens station, right there at the theme park with its rides and shows and little pocket Serengeti for all the Euros who are happy getting a mock Africa thrown into their Florida holiday. Grandpa took Sean-Tomas and his brother there once, fifteen years ago, back when locals could still afford to go.

As they enter the station, Sean-Tomas is remembering little snatches from that day—a giraffe eating leaves, some performing monkeys, a thrilling triple-loop roller coaster, and all the people, the happy, smiling people.

Grandpa's already a little tired. It took the two of them an hour just to get to the glossy, top-techie station with its holo ads and its gift shops full of authentic Florida handicrafts and its fancy restaurant with authentic Florida seafood and its indoor waterfall.

The rackety beat-up local bus seemed to stop at every corner on the way, and the ride was a little risky, too, getting through the neighborhoods in this part of town. But nobody much is gonna mess with somebody the size of Sean-Tomas, Grandpa figures, and here they are, big as life, just like the tourists, riding on out to the Zone in real style, impressive as hell.

Grandpa's dressed in his best—the brown slacks that are twenty, no twenty-five years old now but still look good, and his favorite yellow shirt, and the string tie with the Bucs clasp from the Superbowl back in '98. Some times they had back then, Grandpa thinks. Some times.

Sean-Tomas is dressed up, too, and nervous. It's his first time on the high-speed maglev monorail. This pod is almost empty, but he's listening in on a conversation that four French tourists are having over on the other side. They're having a good time, "bon temps," but they'd like to find a decent meal. And it's too bad, they're saying, that they can't really travel around and see the way people live here. One, the oldest one, with gray hair and a tattered gray beret, can recall when you still could, when the roads were safe enough and everything wasn't yet all closed off for security.

Sean-Tomas can recall those days. But, like his memories of the Gardens, they're all in bits and pieces. He was just a kid when the subdivisions went to hiring the armed guards full-time and putting the broken glass into the concrete walls they were building to shelter themselves from the growing collapse and even, in some places, the rising water.

He can remember walking by a place like that with Raffy. The wall went on forever, and then there was a black steel gate. Two kids, a boy and girl, were on the inside, looking out. Sean and Raffy just walked on by them. Nobody said anything.

Those insiders, the Wallys, still got to live a good reproduction of the good life. The rest, the vast majority, had to deal with reality's decline.

Sean-Tomas can even recall how the attacks finally came. Too few seemed to have too much and the outsiders got upset about it enough to storm OakHaven up in the fancy Carrollwood area and The Trace in comfortable Temple Terrace, not far from where Sean-Tomas lives now. OakHaven fell and was looted, thirty people died. The Trace held and later built a statue to the victory.

But all that was awhile ago. Years. Things are stable now. The adjustment's been made. Violent, deadly sometimes, but stable. Sean-Tomas hasn't really known it any other way.

But Grandpa has. Grandpa remembers how it was and how it all came to be this miserable.

"The price we've all paid," he mumbles to himself as he sits next to Sean-Tomas and stares out the window as the hovels and the occasional high-walled tracts stream by.

"What did you say, Grandpa?" Sean-Tomas asks, only half paying attention. He can't get over how fast they're getting to the Zone. He's walked to it before, just up to the main gate so he could say he'd seen it, and it took him all day. Even on the buses it takes hours. The 'rail is getting them there in maybe fifteen minutes. Amazing. And the tourists consider it all just the normal kit, business as usual.

Downtown Tampa slips by. To Sean-Tomas the water halfway up the first story of downtown's aging skyscrapers is normal. The water taxis get the job done, and there are skyways between buildings. No big deal.

There's never been any trouble handling the water unless there's a big storm. More of those, of course, what with the Greenhouse warming up the water. Sean-Tomas has studied all this, how the storms are forty percent stronger than they used to be, how there's more of them, and how the icecaps are melting and all of that. The gutted old bank building is proof of what the storms can do when they sweep up the coast.

They haven't started rebuilding the thirty-story building, and it's been four years since Miriam roared through. None of the Euros want to fund it; they're in a recession right now and Eurocoin is tight. The city is hoping the Japanese will want to buy in a little more now. The sub-orbital makes Tampa so handy to them, just three and a half hours and they're here.

"... way it used to be," Grandpa is saying. Sean-Tomas hasn't been listening, he's been gawking. He looks away from his own reflection in the tinted glass of the window and smiles at Grandpa.

"The way it used to be," Grandpa says to him again. "It was, well ... hell, we were a great country back then, back before it all fell apart, before the oil dried up and the damn water rose and the Japanese bought everything up and the Euros got together and then went to damn Mars ..."

Sean-Tomas pats his grandfather's arm, stops him. He's seen him get like this before, get all wound up. A lot of the older folks do this, remember how it was and how it all got thrown away and how fast it all came tumbling down when the debts got called in. Sean-Tomas has studied it all, dry and boring, in university.

So what, he figures. Assyria, Egypt, Greece, Rome, Islam, Spain, the French and the British and the Dutch and the Germans and Russians and all the rest. And now us. Empires fall. That's the way it is. Boring dates. Boring names.

All that matters, all that really matters, is passing the European Finals, getting into the Zone where life serving the tourists is easy and you're well fed and taken care of. Sean-Tomas wants to keep the focus narrow, he needs to. Now is not the time for a broad perspective on the national decline and how it could have been stopped or eased. Now is not even the time to worry about Grandpa's whole generation and how they're going to survive with the collapsing empty sack of Social Security. They're sixty-five percent of the population now, they'll figure something out.

Sean-Tomas figures those kind of solutions are out of his control. The Finals, those he can worry about, do something about. The Finals.

They reach the station, arcing in over a lower class hotel that caters to the U.S. trade and then shooting by the remnants of the old interstate bridge. From their height Sean-Tomas can see the whole area better than he ever has before — the hotels stretching north and south into the distance, the huge filter pumps and the barrier booms offshore to clarify the water, the reverse osmosis plant right inside the gate where they make their own fresh water for the tourists, the broken pieces of the interstate bridge marching so visibly across the bay that he thinks it must be low tide.

And there, in the distance, the scattered Pinellas islands, some of them really big. A dozen different tourist boats are in the bay, all of them either heading toward the islands or coming from them. Great fishing over there in the underwater ruins, and the snorkeling in the shallow water is world famous.

Then the 'rail dips down into the station and clicks smoothly into the receiving tube with a gentle bump.

"We're here, boy," says Grandpa, smiling. "The Tourist Zone. Let's go."

They rise, they go, Sean-Tomas almost in a trance. He's actually getting inside.

III

And he's disneyed, absolutely disneyed, by it all. Even the holo ads that flow by in the breeze are new to him. He's fractaled, wiped, burned and blown — every word he can think of to describe it. It's wonderful.

He and Grandpa are getting some stares. No, a lot of stares. Must be the way they're dressed or something. No matter.

They get a bowl of soup, which is all they can really afford, at a restaurant near the docks where the tour boats tie up. Sean-Tomas orders in French and chats with the couple at the next table in Italian. He's in heaven. It's all worth it. He can't wait to really get here.

The couple smiles condescendingly. Yes, they're having a good time. No, they're not sure who they're voting for now that the government has fallen again in Italy. They're Romans, and they don't really care about such matters. Yes, he does speak excellent Italian, something of a northern accent, his teacher must have been from Torino, perhaps. One can hear the mountains in the way he says his "E's."

Then, later, Sean-Tomas and his grandfather walk along the beach. The gurgle of the filter pumps sounds comforting, somehow, Sean-Tomas thinks. They sound like prosperity, like jobs and money and a future.

The beach is narrow, and the Zone Commission will have to bring in more sand from the central part of the state again to widen it out. This happens every year now, Grandpa is thinking as he pokes at a shell with the cane. He does have to wonder how long it can all go on.

Grandpa is really feeling tired now, and something else, too. There's something nagging at him, something he can't quite define yet. There's a feeling, somehow, that he's been here before. But, of course, he hasn't, not since it was zoned for the tourists anyway, and that's been fifteen years now.

It's been a good day for the boy, Grandpa thinks, and worth all the trouble to make it happen. It cost Grandpa what money he had, plus calling in old favors, hocking the Sugar Bowl ring, some begging, some cajoling.

But worth it. Here they are, looking for a good spot on this beach to see the sub-orbital landing. The boy has a future here, a real chance. It's been worth it.

Still, there is this disquieting feeling. Grandpa shakes it off, angrily stabs the cane down onto another shell. The shell shatters.

There is a distant whine. Sean-Tomas hears it first, stops, looks up, scanning the deepening blue of the late afternoon sky for the sub-orbital. Can't see it yet.

Grandpa doesn't look up, he just looks at the boy. Could've been a Gator, maybe.

The whine grows louder. Grandpa finally does look. There, over there, is a glint of sun off those new top-techie tiles that coat the thing. A planeload of Japanese. From there to here in three and one half hours. The next wave of tourists, with pockets full of yen. Spendable yen. Eurocoin and yen, keeping Florida afloat.

A little group of Euros is walking by. Germans. They stop, look up, too, and point.

"Guten tag," says Sean-Tomas, smiling.

The Germans just look back, then look at one another. They smile tightly and begin to move away. Sean-Tomas and his grandfather worry them. They've heard what the locals are like. They're surprised that any of them are allowed on this beach. They'll rob you, they'll beg, they're violent, mean, and stupid. Best just to walk calmly away. Show no fear.

And Grandpa realizes what the feeling is that he's having. He's remembering how it was when he was Sean-Tomas' age or a bit older, when he and Kyoshi were newly married.

They traveled back then, back when you still could, back when there was money for it. The Caribbean, mainly. Jamaica, the Yucatan. Good times, happy times, walking along the beaches, drinks in hand.

And he remembers how they felt about the locals, about the Mexicans, the Jamaicans, about how he and Kyo mainly stayed right in the resort area. What did they call it in Cancun? The Hotel Zone, that was it. And the warning signs in Negril about leaving the resort's beach. "Beware peddlers."

The whine is a roar now. Sean-Tomas is speechless, stunned by the sight and sound of the sub-orbital heading for the runway, retractable wings fully extended, landing gear down, scramjets silent as the propfans ease the huge thing toward the ground.

Grandpa stares as it passes by, its huge shadow going right over them. He just stares, and then turns to leave.

Sean-Tomas is excited. He doesn't understand why Grandpa's gotten so quiet, sullen almost. The older folks, Sean-Tomas thinks sadly to himself. It's tough on them.

And then he turns his thoughts again to the Finals, to his German verbs, to his future as he watches the sub-orbital gently touch down.

QUESTIONS FOR CRITICAL THINKING AND WRITING

1. How does Sean-Tomas explain the odd behavior of the other tourists in the Zone? What is the actual explanation, and how is it revealed?

2. What is the significance of the names in the story? How else does Wilber use language to signify major shifts in society without actually describing an event?

3. How is the character of Sean-Tomas portrayed? Is he intelligent? Proactive? Naive? What makes you assign these characteristics to him?

4. **CONNECT TO ANOTHER READING.** Dave Barry's "The Walt 'You Will Have Fun' Disney World Themed Shopping Complex and Resort Compound" (p. 13) describes the modern state of Disney World and the surrounding adventure parks in Orlando. How are some of the details in Barry's essay parallel to those in Rick Wilber's story? What other similarities do you see between Barry's essay and Wilber's story?

JOHN M. WILLIAMS AND IVER W. DUEDALL

John M. Williams has worked at the National Hurricane Center in Coral Gables, Florida, and as a research affiliate for the Florida Institute of Technology, Melbourne. He previously served in the U.S. Army as a staff officer who specialized in satellite and tropical meteorology.

Iver W. Duedall is a professor of environmental sciences and oceanography at the Florida Institute of Technology. He received his Ph.D. from Dalhousie University in Halifax, Nova Scotia, and currently specializes in the study of ocean pollution and waste research.

The following excerpt is from their book, *Florida Hurricanes and Tropical Storms, 1871–2001*.

Tropical storms and hurricanes are a fact of life in Florida. How are these storms part of the culture of the state, and how do residents adjust their lives around them?

On Hurricane Andrew   2002

Hurricane Andrew

Except for several tropical depressions, June, July, and half of August in the 1992 hurricane season were quiet. The last season with a late start had been 1977, with Anita on August 28, in the Gulf of Mexico.

But on August 14, 1992, satellite photos indicated a strong tropical wave off the African coast in the area of the Cape Verde Islands. This system moved west for two days and developed into a tropical depression near 11.6N and 40.4W early on August 17. By noon that day the winds had reached 40 mph and Tropical Storm Andrew was named. Its position was about 1,175 miles east of the Lesser Antilles.

By August 20, Andrew was in trouble. The winds were less than 45 mph and the barometric pressure was that of normal sea level, leaving the whole system shaky. At this point San Juan, Puerto Rico, was only 350 miles southwest of the storm, but Andrew had slowed down.

The next morning, however, winds were up to 60 mph and pressure had dropped to 29.71 inches. By 11:00 that night, Andrew was 610 miles east of Nassau in the Bahamas, with 65 mph winds. On the morning of August 22, air reconnaissance confirmed that "Andrew is now a hurricane." Winds were 76 mph, pressure was 29.35 inches, and the storm was 800 miles east of Miami. At 11:00 that night Andrew was moving dead west at 15 mph with 110 mph winds and a pressure of 28.32 inches—a Category 2 hurricane.

By noon of August 23 Andrew had intensified to become a Category 4 hurricane. Winds were 135 mph, pressure had dropped to 27.46 inches, and the storm was 330 miles east of Miami, still moving west at 16 mph. At 2:25 that afternoon, Andrew was at its peak with 150 mph winds and pressure of 27.23 inches (Andrew came close to being a Category 5 storm). At this point a hurricane watch was posted from Titusville south to Vero Beach, and hurricane warnings covered the area from Vero Beach south through the Keys and up the west coast to Fort Myers.

By 9:00 in the evening on August 23, Andrew was in the Bahamas, 180 miles east of Miami. Landfall near Miami was predicted for the early morning of August 24. Indeed, between 4:00 and 5:00 A.M. that morning Andrew struck the Florida coastline just south of Miami with sustained winds of 145 mph and recorded gusts of 164 mph, as reported by the National Hurricane Center in Coral Gables before the main radar at the center was destroyed [see the photo]. Gusts to 175 mph were later confirmed.

Andrew crossed the state with 125 mph winds and a forward speed of 18 mph, still moving dead west and by now a Category 3 storm. Pressure was 27.91 inches. According to the U.S. Army Corps of Engineers (1993), some recorded gusts in mph were Fowey Rocks (Biscayne Bay), 169; National

Satellite image of Hurricane Andrew traveling across South Florida, 1992.
Courtesy of the State Archives of Florida.

Hurricane Center, 164; Turkey Point Power Plant, 163; Turkey Point Nuclear Power Plant, 160; Miami International Airport, 115; Goodyear Blimp Base at Pompano, 100; Palm Beach International Airport, 54. Once over the warm waters of the Gulf of Mexico, winds returned to 140 mph, back to Category 4.

By 6:00 A.M. on August 25, Andrew was 270 miles southeast of New Orleans, now moving west-northwest at 17 mph. Winds were 140 mph. At 1:00 P.M. that day the storm was 150 miles south of New Orleans, moving west-northwest at 16 mph. Winds were still 140 mph and barometric pressure 27.85 inches.

The storm slowed down to almost stationary 30 miles southeast of Lafayette, Louisiana. Early on the twenty-sixth, winds near New Iberia, Louisiana, were reported to be 115 mph with gusts to 160 mph. Landfall occurred between New Iberia and Lafayette, as a Category 3 hurricane. By noon on August 26 Andrew was downgraded to tropical storm status for the first time since August 22. Near Baton Rouge, Louisiana, up to 10 inches of rain fell and there were 65 mph winds, with tornadoes. The system was in eastern Tennessee by the morning of August 28, trying to merge with a cold front, the remains of the Pacific hurricane Lester. Andrew finally died out in Pennsylvania on August 29, 1992.

On Sabbatical with Hurricane Andrew

After anchoring their 40-foot sailboat named *Sabbatical* in Manatee Bay in the upper Keys, Dr. Thomas Stephens, dean of the School of Aeronautics at the Florida Institute of Technology in Melbourne, and his wife, Lois, took refuge in a friend's home in southwest Miami. The following eyewitness account is by Lois Stephens.

Sleep was difficult, but I think we all managed to sleep some. About 2 A.M. it started. The wind was howling and shutters were banging. The five of us all crowded into the hallway, just like the usual pre-hurricane instructions stated. Fortunately, Karen had put out candles for us. So far, so good.

The lights went out; the rain started. The wind got many times stronger and the house almost shivered. The force became so great we ran almost panicky into the bathrooms. There were two, both without windows. Ron and Karen headed for one, Lee, Tom, and I the other. We sat on lawn chairs, nestled close together, in the dark with our eyes closed. We opened the door only long enough to get a small votive candle, but the force became too great to open it. The wind grew more ferocious. Suddenly, the windows began to blow out, one at a time, fiercely smashing against the tiled floors. One huge crash I assumed to be the TV, but it was the newly purchased computer. Glass kept smashing. I had been aware for some time of my two root canals. It was strange, but the teeth had piercing pain. I remembered once before being in an airplane with inadequate pressure regulation and experiencing the same pain. Then it hit.

The drop in pressure in the house was so intense it caused pain in your ears and you had to keep swallowing, something like when a plane takes off, but much, much worse. We tried to open the bathroom door, but the force was too great. So three and two of us sat in silence, eyes closed, waiting for the horror to end. The small door to the "attic" storage space blew in and the rain followed. Water crept in around our feet, and I had a dread of it rising. But it did not. Sometime after 6:00, I think, the wind subsided substantially, and we had nerve enough to leave our sanctuary.

The house was all but demolished. The bed where Tom and I had slept a few hours before was full of glass and wet soggy debris. (My emergency bag of clothing, etc., was waterproof, but I had left it unzipped so it was likewise wet and full of junk.) The newly tiled (and in three rooms, newly carpeted) floors were covered with roof shingles, nails, much glass of all sizes, furniture, books, and of course, with a couple of inches of water. Ceiling fans still clung to their mountings, but under each, the light globes were full of dirty water. Water oozed from holes in the walls where Karen's newly framed tropical paintings had been hung (she is an artist). Paint was stripped from the walls. The carport (a sturdy "permanent" one) and door overhang were gone. The new roof was without shingles, and had gaping holes. A look outside showed that all trees and fences were down.

It was, of course, light now, so being cautious but ignoring some of the warnings we had heard, we walked around the neighborhood. It was sickening, horrifying. Not one house had escaped major damage. Trees, even the largest, were sprawled over houses, cars, and streets. Some cars had only broken windows and dents (as did our friend's), and some were blown about and overturned. One had burned from a fallen power line. Not just the power lines were down, but heavy-duty power poles were also broken. Except for no smoke or fires at this point, it must have been what a "bombed out" area looks like in wartime.

Miraculously, quick checks with neighbors found no one injured. Since roads in every direction were impassable, any hope of getting back to what might or might not be left of our boat were given up for the present.

[Later] Highways were somewhat clear by this time, except for some questionable power lines. Trees and large downed poles lined the way. What was most amazing, though, was that literally thousands of cars had found their way to the same area where we were. Traffic was next to impossible, lights and signs inoperative, and cars in extremely questionable condition. We'll never know the number of traffic accidents that day alone.

We passed the hotel, the Holiday Inn, where we had tried so desperately to get a room. It was standing, but barely, with all windows, balconies, etc., blown away. We passed houses with walls only and houses without any walls. Devastation went on for miles. We passed lines of hundreds of people waiting for water. Huge trucks had apparently been placed there at some point to distribute bottled water. One truck had blown uselessly on its side.

Eventually we got to our boat—it was not where we had left it, of course, but it looked good and was tightly nestled back in a grove of mangroves, aground. Miraculously, even the little Zodiac dinghy was still tied to it, snuggled alongside like a loyal puppy nestled against its master. A window was out, glass was everywhere, and branches were entwined in some lines. A stanchion (Tom says) was out and leaves and red mud covered one side of the boat. It was beautiful—we were ecstatic. The carpet was wet—the galley was soaked and covered with glass, but everything else was as we left it.

That night, Tom and I were alone in the middle of Manatee Bay, the most beautiful anchorage of our entire sailing experience.

The sky was clear and bursting with stars with no electric lights to distract from their beauty. There were no airplanes, distant cars, trains, or any noises. The most amazing phenomenon was taking place in the water around us. We had seen luminous fish on occasion, but we saw intensely brilliant green fish swimming around the boat. We dropped a line in the water and swirled it around and it left a trail of light behind it, somewhat like a comet. If we splashed the water, we splashed thousands of tiny lights. (All of this, of course, sent us later to our reference books to see what we had discovered.) We were so fortunate, so thankful, and we sipped our champagne.

[The next day] We were stopped by the Miami Police in a huge inflatable boat and advised we were on the Coast Guard "list" (missing persons and boats) and to call home.

Andrew Epilogue

The death toll in Hurricane Andrew was 24, far less than has occurred in past hurricanes of comparable strength. Massive evacuations ordered in Florida and Louisiana account for the low death rate.

Hurricane Andrew was the most destructive natural disaster in U.S. history. Damage estimates outstripped $30 billion, most of the property losses being in southern Dade and Monroe counties, from Kendall southward to Key Largo; for the Bahamas the damage was estimated at $250 million and for Louisiana more than $1 billion. In Dade County 90 percent of all homes had major roof damage (U.S. Army Corps of Engineers, 1993), and 117,000 homes were destroyed or had major damage.

According to the U.S. Army Corps of Engineers, who worked cooperatively with other agencies to determine environmental impacts, 12.7 million cubic yards of debris resulting from Andrew were hauled away; there were 39 approved debris-burning sites. Florida's agricultural industry loss alone came to $1.04 billion. There was also moderate impact damage to the offshore reef areas down to a depth of 75 feet (U.S. Army Corps of Engineers, 1993).

Damage to the Turkey Point nuclear power plant belonging to Florida Power and Light Company was $100 million (U.S. Army Corps of Engineers, 1993). As to moored recreational vessels within Biscayne Bay, a total of 918 hurricane-damaged vessels were found; "roughly . . . one-third of the damaged vessels were completely or partially submerged, damaged but floating, and damaged aground" (Antonini et al., 1993). The site of the greatest devastation was in the area of Dinner Key Marina near Coral Gables in Miami.

The recovery process is still under way, but it should be emphasized that the results of tremendous structural damage by Andrew's winds could become cumulative in the future.

Andrew was a compact system with maximum winds occurring in a radius of only about 12 miles. A larger system or one with a landfall a few miles farther north would have been even more catastrophic, affecting the more heavily populated areas of Greater Miami, Miami Beach, and Fort Lauderdale. New Orleans could also have fared much worse than it did.

. . . Hurricane Andrew chalked up some weather records. The 16.9-foot storm tide in Biscayne Bay was a record maximum for southeast Florida. Louisiana had 7-foot storm tides. In the twentieth century, only Hurricane Camille in 1969 and the Great Labor Day Hurricane of 1935 in the Florida Keys had lower barometric pressures at landfall. Barometric pressure associated with Andrew bottomed out at 27.23 inches.

Andrew broke wind speed records. A maximum 10-second flight-level wind speed of 170 knots, or 196 mph, was reported by the reconnaissance aircraft in the vicinity of northern Eleuthera Island in the Bahamas on August 23. The storm surge there was 23 feet.

Andrew will not be the last hurricane to cause such massive devastation and havoc. A similar storm could appear next year, or ten years from now; there is no way to know when. However, the bitter lessons learned in Hurricane Andrew should provide us with ample experience to survive the next big one.

REFERENCES

Antonini, G. A., P. W. Box, M. Clarke, E. Brady, R. Ledesma, and J. L. Rahn. 1993. Location and Assessment of Hurricane Andrew Damaged Vessels on Biscayne Bay and Adjoining Shore Areas. Florida Sea Grant College Program, Gainesville, FL. 58 pp.

U.S. Army Corps of Engineers. 1993. Hurricane Andrew Storm Summary and Impacts on the Beaches of Florida. Special Report. Jacksonville District, Florida. 61 pages plus several appendices.

QUESTIONS FOR CRITICAL THINKING AND WRITING

1. How does the language in the section "Hurricane Andrew" differ from the language in "On Sabbatical with Hurricane Andrew"? What type of language do you prefer, and which do you think was more effective in getting its intended message across to readers?

2. In the section "On Sabbatical with Hurricane Andrew," Lois Stephens describes what was "the most beautiful anchorage of [her] entire sailing experience." What made the anchorage so spectacular? Do you believe

her experience of the hurricane was typical of other residents'? Why or why not?

3. **CONNECT TO ANOTHER READING.** How does the description of the awful power of nature in "On Hurricane Andrew" compare to the portrayal of nature in Stephen Crane's "The Open Boat" (p. 32)? Do the authors come to similar conclusions about nature? What are those conclusions, and how are they reached by each author?

TENNESSEE WILLIAMS

Tennessee Williams (1911–1983) is best known as a playwright, and his much-acclaimed works include *A Streetcar Named Desire* and *The Glass Menagerie*. He also adapted many of his plays to the screen, and he won a New York Film Critics' Circle award for the film version of *The Glass Menagerie*. Although he spent much of his professional life in New York, he lived in Florida briefly, and the poem "The Diving Bell" is set in the Florida Keys.

Courtesy of Gjon Mili/Time & Life Pictures/Getty Images.

BEFORE YOU READ

It is always good practice to read a poem at least twice through to fully grasp the meaning, especially in a dense work like "The Diving Bell." As you read through the second (or third) time, take note of the elements you missed the first time around. What images, words, or phrases stand out to you more upon rereading? Why do you think they become more apparent?

The Diving Bell   1977

I want to go under the sea in a diving-bell
and return to the surface with ominous wonders to tell.
I want to be able to say:
   "The base is unstable, it's probably unable
    to weather much weather,   5
being all hung together by a couple of blond hairs caught
in a fine-toothed comb."

I want to be able to say through a P.A. system,
authority giving a sonorous tone to the vowels,
   "I'm speaking from Neptune's bowels.   10
   The sea's floor is nacreous, filmy
with milk in the wind, the light of an overcast morning."

I want to give warning:
   "The pediment of our land is a lady's comb,
   the basement is moored to the dome   15
by a pair of blond hairs caught in a delicate
tortoise-shell comb."

I think it is safer to roam
   than to stay in a mortgaged home
      And so—   20

I want to go under the sea in a bubble of glass
containing a sofa upholstered in green corduroy
and a girl for practical purposes and a boy
   well-versed in the classics.

I want to be first to go down there where action is slow   25
   but thought is surprisingly quick.
   It's only a dare-devil's trick,
   the length of a burning wick
   between tu-whit and tu-who!

   Oh, it's pretty and blue   30
but not at all to be trusted. No matter how deep you go
there's not very much below
   the deceptive shimmer and glow
   which is all for show
of sunken galleons encrusted with barnacles and doubloons,   35
an undersea tango palace with instant come and
   go moons . . .

QUESTIONS FOR CRITICAL THINKING AND WRITING

1. Williams uses the image of a "fine-toothed comb" with "a couple of blond hairs caught" in it twice in the poem. What might this image represent?
2. What do you think Williams means by the lines "I think it is safer to roam / than to stay in a mortgaged home"?
3. The way the poem appears visually on the page is unusual and interesting. Why do you think Williams chose to have the poem appear this way? Is there significance to the lines that are indented versus those that are not?

Acknowledgments (continued from p. iv)

"All My Sins Been Taken Away" from *Folksongs of Florida*, collected and edited by Alton C. Morris. University of Florida Press, 1950; reprinted 1990. Reprinted with permission of the University Press of Florida.

Dave Barry. "The Walt 'You Will Have Fun' Disney World Themed Shopping Complex and Resort Compound" from *Dave Barry's Only Travel Guide You'll Ever Need* by Dave Barry. Copyright © 1989 by Dave Barry. Used by permission of Ballantine Books, a division of Random House, Inc. Any third party use of this material, outside of this publication, is prohibited. Interested parties must apply directly to Random House, Inc., for permission.

Elizabeth Bishop. "The Bight" from *The Complete Poems, 1927–1979* by Elizabeth Bishop. Copyright © 1979, 1983 by Alice Helen Methfessel. Reprinted by permission of Farrar, Straus and Giroux, LLC.

Jimmy Buffett. "Hooked in the Heart" from *Tales from Margaritaville* by Jimmy Buffett. Copyright © 1989 by Jimmy Buffett. Reprinted by permission of Houghton Mifflin Harcourt Publishing Company. All rights reserved.

Susan Cerulean. "'Restorying' Florida" from *The Wild Heart of Florida*, edited by Jeffrey S. Ripple and Susan Cerulean. University Press of Florida, 1999. Reprinted with permission of the University Press of Florida.

"Come and Jine" from *Folksongs of Florida*, collected and edited by Alton C. Morris. University of Florida Press, 1950; reprinted 1990. Reprinted with permission of the University Press of Florida.

Betty Sue Cummings. Excerpt from *Say These Names (Remember Them)* by Betty Sue Cummings. Copyright © 1984 by Betty Sue Cummings. Reprinted by permission.

Silvia Curbelo. "For All the Goodbyes" from *The Secret History of Water* by Silvia Curbelo (Anhinga Press, 1997). Copyright © 1997 by Silvia Curbelo. Reprinted by permission of the author.

Joan Didion. Chapter 3 of *Miami* by Joan Didion. Copyright © 1987 by Joan Didion. Reprinted by permission of the author.

Ernest Hemingway. Chapter Twenty of *To Have and Have Not* by Ernest Hemingway. Copyright © 1937 by Ernest Hemingway. Copyright renewed © 1965 by Mary Hemingway. Copyright © 1934 by Hearst Magazines, Inc. Copyright renewed © 1962 by Mary Hemingway. Reprinted with the permission of Scribner, a division of Simon & Schuster, Inc. All rights reserved.

Carl Hiaasen. Excerpt from *Chomp* by Carl Hiaasen. Copyright © 2012 by Carl Hiaasen. Used by permission of Alfred A. Knopf, an imprint of Random House Children's Books, a division of Random House, Inc. Any third party use of this material, outside of this publication, is prohibited. Interested parties must apply directly to Random House, Inc., for permission.

Carolina Hospital. "How the Cubans Stole Miami" was first published by *Prairie Schooner*, Winter 1994. Copyright © 1994 by Carolina Hospital. Reprinted by permission of the author.

Zora Neale Hurston. Excerpt from *Mules and Men* by Zora Neale Hurston. Copyright © 1935 by Zora Neale Hurston. Renewed 1963 by John C. Hurston and Joel Hurston. Reprinted by permission of HarperCollins Publishers.

Gloria Jahoda. Excerpt from Chapter 4, "The Garden of Eden," in *The Other Florida* by Gloria Jahoda. Copyright © 1967 by Gloria Jahoda. Reprinted with the permission of Scribner, a division of Simon & Schuster, Inc. All rights reserved.

Gloria Jahoda. Excerpt from "Marshes and Moonports" in *Florida: A Bicentennial History* by Gloria Jahoda. Copyright © 1976 by the American Association for State and Local History. Used by permission of W. W. Norton & Company, Inc.

"The Jolly Bachelor" from *Folksongs of Florida*, collected and edited by Alton C. Morris. University of Florida Press, 1950; reprinted 1990. Reprinted with permission of the University Press of Florida.

Jeff Klinkenberg. "Brooker Creek" from *The Wild Heart of Florida*, edited by Jeffrey S. Ripple and Susan Cerulean. University Press of Florida, 1999. Reprinted with permission of the University Press of Florida.

"Larger Than Life" from *Florida Folktales*, edited by J. Russell Reaver. University Presses of Florida/University of Florida Press, 1987. Reprinted with permission of the University Press of Florida.

Index of Authors and Titles

More composition help online, 24/7
bedfordstmartins.com/rewriting

Re:writing
Bedford/St. Martin's

To get the full value out of this book and this course, visit *Re:Writing*. It's completely free. Why not use it?

Watch videos of real writers.

See reliable research links.

Try a tutorial on avoiding plagiarism [or analyzing visuals].

See sample documents in design.

Find help with citing sources.

Build a bibliography.

Find checklists for better writing.

Try exercises for grammar and writing.

Create a study plan for grammar and writing.